SALTWATER
LEADERSHIP

TITLES IN THE SERIES

THE U.S. NAVAL INSTITUTE
BLUE & GOLD PROFESSIONAL LIBRARY

FOR MORE THAN 100 YEARS, U.S. NAVY PROFESSIONALS have counted on specialized books published by the Naval Institute Press to prepare them for their responsibilities as they advance in their careers and to serve as ready references and refreshers when needed. From the days of coal-fired battleships to the era of unmanned aerial vehicles and laser weaponry, such perennials as *The Bluejacket's Manual* and the *Watch Officer's Guide* have guided generations of Sailors through the complex challenges of naval service. As these books are updated and new ones are added to the list, they will carry the distinctive mark of the Blue & Gold Professional Library series to remind and reassure their users that they have been prepared by naval professionals and meet the exacting standards that Sailors have long expected from the U.S. Naval Institute.

BLUE & GOLD
PROFESSIONAL LIBRARY

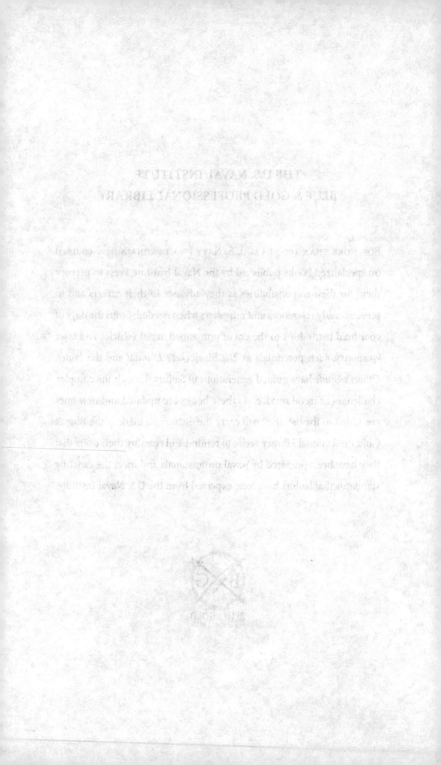

SALTWATER LEADERSHIP

SECOND EDITION

A Primer on Leadership for the Sea Services

RADM Robert O. Wray Jr., USN (Ret.)
CDR Andrew K. Ledford, USN, PhD
VADM John B. Mustin, USN
RDML Theodore P. S. LeClair, USN

Naval Institute Press
291 Wood Road
Annapolis, MD 21402

Library of Congress Cataloging-in-Publication Data
Names: Wray, Robert O., Jr., author.
Title: Saltwater leadership : a primer on leadership for the sea services /
  RADM Robert O. Wray Jr., USN (Ret.); CDR Andrew K. Ledford, USN;
RADM
  John B. Mustin, USN; and RDML Ted LeClair, USN.
Other titles: Primer on leadership for the sea services
Description: Second edition. | Annapolis, MD : Naval Institute Press,
  [2021] | Series: The U.S. Naval Institute blue & gold professional
  library | Includes bibliographical references and index.
Identifiers: LCCN 2020050479 (print) | LCCN 2020050480 (ebook) | ISBN
  9781682475508 (paperback) | ISBN 9781682476383 (ebook) | ISBN
  9781682476383 (pdf)
Subjects: LCSH: United States. Navy—Officers' handbooks. | Merchant
  marine—United States—Officers—Handbooks, manuals, etc. |
  Leadership—Handbooks, manuals, etc. | United States. Navy—Sea
  life—Anecdotes. | Naval art and science—Handbooks, manuals, etc.
Classification: LCC V133 .W73 2021 (print) | LCC V133 (ebook) | DDC
  359.3/3041—dc23
LC record available at https://lccn.loc.gov/2020050479
LC ebook record available at https://lccn.loc.gov/2020050480

♾ Print editions meet the requirements of ANSI/NISO z39.48-1992
(Permanence of Paper).
Printed in the United States of America.

29 28 27 26 25 24 23 22   9 8 7 6 5 4 3

This book is dedicated to all those who go to sea
and to those who lead them.

One hundred percent of the royalties from this book
will be donated to charities that support Sailors and mariners,
including the Navy and Marine Corps Relief Society,
the Coast Guard Foundation, and the United Seaman's Service.

CONTENTS

CONTENTS

FOREWORD TO THE FIRST EDITION

From the maxims of Publilius Syrus to the insights of Dale Carnegie, the rhumb lines of Arleigh Burke to the contemporary advice of James Stavridis, *Saltwater Leadership* contains lessons from the most revered thought-leaders and valued sources and condenses them into chapters that you can absorb and understand between watches or sorties. *Saltwater Leadership* will provide you with the insights of hundreds of senior sea service leaders and the instruments to chart a course toward your own leadership horizon.

A lesson in leadership that has influenced me throughout my life came from my grandfather, Admiral John S. McCain Sr., who commanded a carrier task force in the Pacific during World War II. After pilots returned from strikes he would seek them out, asking them, 'Do you think we're doing the right thing?' He knew that if he ever stopped learning from his men, then he stopped leading.

Whether exercised in self-discipline or over the forces of a combatant command, leadership is vital, and the challenges and opportunities of the future demand it. I hope you take these lessons to heart—in my experience, the wisdom in these pages can give you strength and hope during the most challenging of times.

John McCain
United States Senator

PREFACE

The word "primer," according to *Webster's Dictionary*, is "a small introductory book on a subject," from the Medieval Latin *primarium*. This book is intended as a primer. In no way does it deserve to sit alongside such seminal leadership texts as Karel Montor's *Naval Leadership*, which took dozens of people dozens of years to produce. It is intended as a short, simple book that can be read in five-minute snippets by a busy young officer at sea.

Much of the material in this book is Navy-centric. This has three causes: First, the authors have served in the Navy, collectively, for over 110 years, and many of the contributors to this book responded because they knew us from prior service together. Second, due to its size, the Navy has more officers serving at sea today than either the Coast Guard or the U.S. Merchant Marine, so a preponderance of officers-at-sea stories come from that greater population. And third, the Navy has been more prolific in the generation of books about leadership than either the Coast Guard or Merchant Marine. Because this book provides an overview of some of the existing literature, its content therefore becomes more Navy-oriented. In any case, this is a book for junior officers at sea, regardless of service type, community, or agency. We have attempted to make the stories and lessons applicable to all, regardless of the source. We believe any young graduate from Kings Point can learn a lesson from a Coast Guard cutter in the Caribbean, just as a graduate from an NROTC unit can learn seagoing lessons from deep-draft tankers in Alaskan waters.

Finally, we would like to acknowledge the contributions of CDR David Wallace of the USNA Leadership Department for his contributions to chapter 2.

—*RADM Robert O. Wray Jr., USN (Ret.)*
—*CDR Andrew K. Ledford, USN, PhD*
—*VADM John B. Mustin, USN*
—*RDML Theodore P. S. LeClair, USN*

INTRODUCTION

⚓

This book is about leadership, written for leaders at sea. It is not intended to be an academic text. As you'll see, it's certainly not a work of literature. It is intended to be functional, simple, down to earth, easy to digest, and straightforward, communicating basic truths without frills.

Leadership deals with the very nature of humanity, with what we are here for, with how we should interact with other humans, with what we should do in this world. It is a serious matter. Some books on leadership necessarily deal with the philosophic and existential issues of why humans do what we do and how we do it. Leadership strikes at the heart of humanity and vice versa. It can be a satisfying and worthwhile study.

Other books focus on the more pedestrian, more pragmatic views of leadership. What is it? How can we describe it? How can we identify the successful ways of leadership? And, more importantly, how can we become successful leaders?

This book focuses on the latter view, specifically for leaders at sea. The authors have been where you are—we know your busy life might not leave room for reading the classic texts cover to cover to learn leadership. Instead, this book attempts to offer you simple leadership lessons in bite-sized chunks that can be consumed and digested between watches and sea evolutions, during the few minutes each day that you might have to yourself. Perhaps the small chunks provided here will whet your appetite.

Given that limited aim, we hope this book meets the mark for you.

CHAPTER 1

LEADERSHIP FOR YOUNG
LEADERS AT SEA

A leader is best
When people barely know that he exists,
Not so good when people obey and acclaim him,
Worst when they despise him.

"Fail to honor people,
They fail to honor you";

But of a good leader, who talks little,
When his work is done, his aim fulfilled,
They will all say, "We did this ourselves."
—Lao Tzu, Tao Teh Ching,
verse 17, 6th century BC

This is the bottom line, right here, up front, on the first page:

Leadership matters. Everything of value in the world happens because of leadership.

Leadership is definable. It's not some hocus-pocus, touchy-feely amorphous state of mind or relationship. It can be described and defined. It can be measured.

You can be a leader. It's learnable. You don't have to be born with it. Whatever you are today, you can become a better leader tomorrow, if you choose.

You, too, can make things happen.

Winston Churchill said, in writing to young officers like you: "Come on now all you young people all over the world. You have not an hour to lose. You must take your place in Life's fighting line. Twenty to twenty five! Those are the years. Don't be content with things as they are. Don't take No for an answer. Never submit to failure. You will make all kinds of mistakes; but as long as you are generous and true and also fierce, you cannot hurt the world!"

Are you ready to make things happen? Are you ready to be generous and true and fierce?

Are you ready to be a leader?

You can be. Read this book!

THE SIX BASIC QUESTIONS

"What is leadership, anyway?"

A good question, and one that many people have studied for many years. There are a hundred definitions.

Webster's Dictionary defines leadership as "the act of being a leader" and defines a leader as a person "with commanding authority or influence."

According to Navy General Order 21 (as first issued), leadership is defined as "the art of accomplishing the Navy's mission through people." In the Commandant's Instruction on Leadership, the Coast Guard declares that leadership is "the ability to influence others to obtain their obedience, respect, confidence, and loyal cooperation." The Army states that leadership is "influencing people—by providing purpose, direction, and motivation—while operating to accomplish the mission and improving the organization."

In our midshipman-leadership text written several decades ago, leadership was somewhat loftily defined as "the art, science, or gift by which a person is enabled and privileged to direct the thoughts, plans, and actions of others in such a manner as to obtain and command their obedience, their confidence, their respect, and their loyal cooperation."

Field Marshal Bernard Montgomery said, "Leadership is the capacity and will to rally men and women to a common purpose and the character which inspires confidence." Similarly, Dwight Eisenhower remarked, "Leadership is the art of getting someone else to do something you want done because he wants to do it."

> **Leading sailors is an art, not a science.**
> —*ADM Arleigh Burke*

Finally, Harry Truman echoed Eisenhower almost word for word when he said, "A leader is a man who has the ability to get other people to do what they don't want to do, and like it." In other words: *Leadership is the process of getting people to do things.*

Now, that might seem manipulative, crass, and simplistic. Maybe it is. But in the end, things happen only because people make them happen, and someone has to get those people to make them happen. That's where leadership comes in.

"What's the difference between leadership and management?"

Another good question, and one often asked by junior officers. Like anything having to do with leadership, there are plenty of different answers. Some say leadership is deciding *what* to do and *why*, while management focuses on *how*.

> A manager's job is to create stability and deal with reality.
> A leader's job is to stir emotion and set audacious, grandiose
> goals that shake the status quo. Too much management and
> you stagnate. Too much leadership and you get nowhere.
> Embrace the challenge of striking the balance. Do it well,
> and the results will surpass your wildest dreams.
>
> —*The Management and Leadership Network*

Some believe leadership focuses on accomplishing the mission, while management is about doing it efficiently. Management author Ken Adelman says, "A leader knows what's best to do; a manager knows how best to do it."

Others argue that leadership is about influencing, while management is more about operating. But notice that the Army definition of leadership in the section above includes both influencing and operating. Renowned Harvard professor and leadership expert John Kotter says that management is about running things in steady state, while leadership is about causing change.

Management guru Warren Bennis laid out the following distinctions between the two:

- Leaders do the right things; managers do things right.
- Leaders innovate; managers administer.
- Leaders inspire; managers control.
- Leaders think long term; managers think short term.

- Leaders originate; managers imitate.
- Leaders challenge the status quo; managers accept the status quo.

As usual, all these views are right, in their own way. For the junior officer, you will be providing both management and leadership to the folks who work for you, and often the two will overlap. For instance, say you're working on a tough project and one of your key people has a family situation that needs attention. Deciding to let that person go tend to family matters, even if it hurts your team strength, is a leadership decision. Figuring out how to adjust other team schedules to make it work is more about management.

"Why is leadership important?"
In the world of the junior officer, does leadership really matter? Isn't your job really about standing a good watch and managing the few people who might work for you? Leadership is important to you in two ways.

First, it will help you do your job better—today. You are not in charge of three bookkeepers in office cubicles working 9:00 to 5:00 weekdays. Management alone could probably get that job done.

Rather, you are responsible for far more people under far more arduous, difficult, and unpredictable circumstances. You and your team are working 24/7, year-round, in bad weather, in difficult situations, in conflict, sometimes under adversity, or sometimes even under fire. These conditions call for more than management. Your decisions can place your people in danger. Sending a mariner topside at night in freezing foul weather to find and fix a thorny problem isn't management—it takes leadership to have influence like that. Leading a team into a smoke-filled space to put out a fire isn't management; it's leadership, pure and simple.

> I consider it a great advantage to obtain command young, having observed as a general thing that persons who come into authority late in life shrink from responsibility, and often break down under its weight.
> —*ADM David Farragut*

Being a leader is critical to get your job done, even as the most junior officer in your outfit. If you need further evidence, look at your performance evaluation. Is there a block for "management"? Probably not. Is there a block to evaluate you in leadership? Absolutely.

Second, leadership is important to you today because, in most cases, it is the coin of the realm for your advancement in the sea services. The path to the top comprises leadership steps that are critical, without which you'll never progress. Whether your goal is to become a master or chief engineer of a ship, a captain in the Coast Guard or Navy, or the commander of a battalion of Marines, you can't do it without successfully demonstrating leadership at every level as you progress.

"Is leadership innate or learned?"

Leadership is 3 percent innate, 97 percent learned.

Those numbers aren't exact, obviously—they're our view of it; and as you'll find in leadership study, every author has a different point of view. But based on our many, many years of leadership experience and study, that breakdown is pretty close.

Some naturally born elements are helpful. For instance, statistically, being tall appears to help with leadership. The overwhelming majority of presidential elections have been won by the taller candidate. In the corporate marketplace, taller people generally get paid slightly more and are promoted slightly more often. But in a recent meeting of all the Navy admirals in Norfolk, Virginia, the most senior four star was the shortest admiral in the room; the second shortest was his female three-star deputy. So much for height being important nowadays.

Being intelligent also helps. Intelligence can help you be a better communicator and a better solver of problems. It also helps you learn leadership skills faster. There is a positive correlation between intelligence and advancement in corporate-management hierarchies—in other words, senior managers tend to score higher in intelligence tests than middle managers. Similarly, chief executives are, in general, measurably smarter than senior managers.

Finally, for some circumstances, it helps to be big and strong. In some groups, size and strength can assist in leadership. In most groups or organizations, however, it's immaterial. For most organizations, only your mental strength truly matters. In fact, as you mature through your career in the sea services, you'll find with every passing year that you're more likely to be paid to *think* than to *do*.

But that's about it for innate qualities. All the other leadership traits—character, speaking ability, empathy, organization, vision, honesty, work ethic, amiability, courage, perseverance—are acquired traits. They are all learned.

They are all available to you. If you didn't get exposed to them growing up, you can learn them now, if you choose.

"How does one become a leader?"

If you wanted to play the piano, what would you do? Most likely, you would

- study a book on music and theory
- take lessons from a teacher
- practice the piano
- watch and listen to others play

If you want to learn French, if you want to become a chef, if you want to hit a curveball—if you want to learn virtually anything—your tasks might include

- studying
- receiving instruction from a teacher
- practicing
- observing others

So it is with leadership. Leadership can be learned using these four basic tenets.

Col Art Athens, a leadership professor at the Naval Academy and former commandant of the Merchant Marine Academy at Kings Point, New York, has written that leadership can be learned through six fundamental building blocks:

- self-knowledge
- observation
- intellectual base

- mentoring
- adversity
- experience

Athens's six building blocks are nouns—they provide the foundation of leadership. Our four items above—studying, receiving instruction, practicing, and observing—are verbs. They are what you, the young leader, can *do* to acquire those six building blocks.

Remember, you can *become* a leader. You can learn. You do it by

- studying leadership
- having a mentor or a teacher who can help you perfect your skills
- practicing and experiencing leadership
- watching other leaders around you, both good and bad

SPOM: Study, Practice, Observe, Mentor. It's not rocket science. But, by the way, if you wanted to learn rocket science, you'd learn it the same way!

Leadership and learning are indispensable to each other.
—*John F. Kennedy*

One note: the four steps above all require one thing. *Will.* You have to *want* to be a leader. You don't become a leader through osmosis or through mere desire. You can desire to be a great piano player, but unless you take the steps to make it happen, it won't happen. ADM William Pratt, former chief of Naval Operations, said: "Few realize that the growth to sound leadership is a life's work. Ambition alone will not encompass it. [It] is a long, hard road to travel."

"Why another book on leadership?"

A very good question. One could argue that the world doesn't need another book on leadership. There are business leadership books and academic leadership books and theoretical leadership books and military leadership books. Why another?

This is the only leadership book written specifically for you young officers in the seagoing services on ships, operating aircraft, leading troops, and defending our homeland in the Navy, Marine Corps, Coast Guard, and the Merchant Marine. Your conditions are different; your needs are different. Leadership lessons and concepts can be universal, but this book is written specifically for you in two ways.

First, the lessons and concepts are placed in the sea-service context in which you lead your lives. You could potentially learn leadership lessons by reading about business leaders or about Air Force officers flying jets, but you'll learn those lessons better if you hear from people who have worn your shoes and lived your life.

Second, the book is written in a format with your life in mind. We know you're busy and tired and not all that interested in reading a nine-hundred-page, footnoted tome about leadership. In your life today, short, sweet, and to the point is better.

So, that's the reason for another leadership book—but one that will hopefully fit your life and needs. And, when your needs go beyond the "Leadership 101" simplicities of this primer, refer to the appendixes when you want to drink more deeply of this vital topic.

HOW THIS BOOK IS ORGANIZED

Think of this short book as comprising three parts:

Chapters 1–3 provide an overview to get you started. First, we introduce the topic and the book. Then, we summarize about three thousand years of thought on leadership into a brief chapter on the history of leadership. In chapter 3, we attempt to drill down further on the definition of leadership. You'll find that there are as many definitions as there are writers and teachers!

In chapters 4–8, we present about one hundred sea stories that illustrate leadership principles. Each is short, easy to read, and provides a clear message and clear takeaways for you. Each is written by a sea-service officer who has "been there, done that." We've binned these many stories into five primary groups:

Junior Officer Leadership
Taking Care of Your People
Forceful Backup
Culture
Professional Competence

In chapters 9 and 10, we close with a consolidated list of leadership advice for the junior officer and some thoughts on how to build your leadership skills to become the leader you want to be—the leader your country needs you to be.

So let's get going!

CHAPTER 2

A BRIEF HISTORY
OF LEADERSHIP

⚓

It is by no means enough that an officer of the Navy be a capable mariner. He must be that, of course, but also a great deal more. He should be as well a gentleman of liberal education, [having] refined manners, punctilious courtesy, and the nicest sense of personal honor.

He should be the soul of tact, patience, justice, firmness, and charity. No meritorious act of a subordinate should escape his attention or be left to pass without its reward, even if the reward is only a word of approval. Conversely, he should not be blind to a single fault in any subordinate, though at the same time, he should be quick and unfailing to distinguish error from malice, thoughtfulness from incompetency, and well-meant shortcoming from heedless or stupid blunder.

In one word, every commander should keep constantly before him the great truth, that to be well obeyed, he must be perfectly esteemed.

—John Paul Jones

Any compendium of leadership should include some acknowledgment of the well-known philosophies available to reveal some manner of how leadership works. Great leaders don't just simply lead. To hone their craft, they study it in the same way great musicians study musical theory to improve their composition or painters study modernist and impressionist art to improve their own technique. The complexity of inspiring a group of free-willed people to align their efforts toward accomplishing a larger goal requires more than a step-by-step process; leaders must be able to apply a mixture of science and art to know both *what* must be done and *how* to do it. It is here that leaders can be informed by a study of leadership and by experiences in which they develop their art. This chapter is designed to whet your appetite with the science of leadership—the *how*. The rest of this book is designed to help you hone your art by reading stories of how others have led—the *what must be done*.

Leadership has been a topic of fictional stories and factual accounts since before there was the written word. Later, Greek and Roman historians such as Herodotus and Thucydides cited feats of leadership often in their accounts of their ancient civilizations. These leadership stories were the blockbuster movies of their time—everyone heard and knew them. Likewise, the wisdom of Eastern writers such as Sun Tzu, Confucius, and Lao Tzu included a great deal of lessons for the savvy leader. *The Art of War* by Sun Tzu advises to "be a leader with vision. To see an opportunity only when it is apparent to everyone is not very impressive, nor is being complimented by everyone for your successes. To lift a small thing requires no great strength, to see only what is right before your face requires no great vision, and to hear the booming roar of thunder requires no great hearing."

IS LEADERSHIP REALLY ABOUT THE "GREAT MAN"?

Such advice has been handed down for many generations, but the modern discipline of leadership starts for the most part in the mid-nineteenth century with a Scottish philosopher, Thomas Carlyle, and his book *On Heroes, Hero-Worship, and the Heroic in History.* This is a key source that is referenced in most modern studies of leadership. Carlyle examines the biographies of great leaders and heroes and suggests that these great men (and only men were examined at that time) were born with certain special traits that made them heroic. This "Great Man" theory, later called the "Trait" theory, suggests that this occurs most often under dire circumstances through which great leaders emerge, defying the odds and vanquishing their foes to achieve great success and victory as if from a Marvel comic. A central tenet of this theory is that there are "right qualities" and "right personalities" that are necessary for great leadership in dire circumstances. This idea has been passed down to the present in the stories we tell of great naval leaders and the accompanying admonitions to "be like" John Paul Jones in his audacity, Churchill in his tenacity, GEN George S. Patton in his courage, or VADM James Stockdale in his integrity.

WHAT TRAITS MAKE UP THE "GREAT MAN"?

Since Carlyle, there have been a great number of studies done to examine which skills and traits are the important ones, because if we could just find the list of the right traits, we could pick the best people (those who possess those qualities) and put them in charge. You may be able to think of a few traits yourself: extroversion, enthusiasm, talkativeness, assertiveness, and gregariousness. One can be an introvert, however, and still be a great, transformational leader: Mahatma Gandhi, Elon Musk, Bill Gates, and Warren Buffett are just a few of many such examples. Charisma, being charming in a way that inspires devotion, surely must be a desirable quality. History, though, has been rife with uncharismatic leaders such as Angela Merkel and John Adams, while a plethora of charismatic leaders were absolute disasters, including Bernie Madoff and Hugo Chávez. In study after study, a harsh truth becomes apparent: there is *no perfect list of skills or traits* that can predict who will be a great leader. Why not? First, great leaders utilize the gifts they already have as leverage against their weaknesses, increase their skills and experience over time, and often rise to the demands of the occasion. Second, the leader is only *one* part of the formula for great leadership. Well, what are the others? Let's find out.

THE *SITUATION* MATTERS, NOT THE TRAITS

One of the other elements that must be studied in leadership is the *specific situation* surrounding the leader. Is leadership in a wartime environment with the danger of enemy contact nearby different from leadership in a division or platoon stationed at home conducting routine maintenance and training? Why is different leadership required? Three researchers, Kenneth Blanchard, Paul Hersey, and Walter Natameyer, have suggested that there really is no "*best* leadership style" and that it's important for leaders to adjust their own style of leadership to the situation, attempting to meet the needs and skills of the group they're trying to influence. Leaders must understand the situation first and foremost. This includes a complete understanding of the task at hand and what is needed to accomplish it; this is their professional competence, or "expertise in the job." It also requires a complete understanding of the team members, including their abilities and motivations. This is "knowing their people." Finally, it requires that a leader has a complete understanding of the external factors that will influence the mission. This is their observation of their environment, their "Spidey-sense" or "eyes in the back of the head." The situation in which both the leader and followers find themselves is a driving factor in how the leader will behave and how each follower will perceive and react to the leader's behaviors.

CAN LEADERS CHANGE THEIR LEADERSHIP STYLE?

In contrast to the Great Man theory, there are some who believe there is no one "correct" leadership style that is applicable to all situations all the time; great leaders appropriate different styles for different occasions. But leaders adapting their own style of leadership to different circumstances, as situational leadership requires, is just one approach. Another researcher, Fred Fiedler, has proposed a different tack to thinking about leadership, called "Contingency Theory to Leadership." This approach suggests matching the leader's style to particular situations, *not* adapting one's style to conditions. For this approach, one's leadership style is fixed and never changes. With this understanding, it's paramount to understand what the leader's particular style is and orient that person to the situation most favorable to that style. Leaders are either mostly task oriented, where there is a formal and somewhat rigid organizational structure in place, or people oriented, where the relationships between the leader and followers are particularly strong and important. Linda Oakleaf explains that the situation can also be analyzed into three similar factors that matter: the rigidity and clarity of the tasks at hand, the leader's relationships with the followers, and the formal and informal power structures of the organization. How the two possibilities of the leader match the three factors of the situation describes the "right fit" within this particular conception of leadership.

The difference between these two approaches is stark. In situational leadership, the leader's ability to adapt personal style to each situation depending on what is required is essential. In contingency theory, a leader is either a "good fit" or a "poor fit" with the situation based on how well that person's style matches what is required. With this approach, leader recruitment and placement is essential to successful leadership. Pairing the "right leader" with the

Leaders: How these fit together defines good leadership or poor leadership **Situation:**

Task oriented → Rigidity/clarity of tasks

or   The relationship with the followers

People oriented   The power structures in the organization

Contingency Theory of Leadership

"right situation" is a crucial function in successful organizations.

Our more modern understanding of leadership is that both theories might be true: leaders must be flexible according to the demands of the situation but also be able to see the opportunities and lean in to their natural strengths. To meet these demands and to take advantage of these opportunities, research shows that leaders must not only develop their own abilities and learn from their own experiences but also surround themselves with others whose strengths complement their own. The imperative for maritime leaders is to:

1. Know yourself.
2. Constantly scan and understand the situation (including the task, your followers, and the environment).
3. Develop your own skills.
4. Rely on others to help.

MORE RECENT THEORIES: TRANSFORMATIONAL, TRANSACTIONAL, AND SERVANT LEADERSHIP

In recent decades, some leadership theorists and popular-press pundits have responded to a sense that perhaps there is "something more" to understanding leadership than a matching of traits and situations—that true leadership is something more than mere management—creating an explosion of theories that try to define what leadership is. Even a cursory search of blogs and business magazines will quickly lead to terms such as "transformational leadership," "servant leadership," and "authentic leadership."

A recent and popular theory proposed by Bernard Bass, called "transformational leadership," suggests that leaders should clearly articulate a bold and inspiring vision, treat followers as individuals with valuable contributions, and challenge the team to innovate and to think in different ways. In doing so, such leaders will inspire those around them to go beyond mundane compliance with orders or directives to achieve full commitment to, well, transformational action.

Another popular view of leadership often discussed in business publications is "servant leadership." Robert Greenleaf suggests that those leaders who focus intently on others—that is, prioritizing the needs and interests of followers and others in the organization and community over their own needs and interests—will garner an organization built on trust and strong relationships.

Finally, Gardner Avolio and May Luthans suggest that with their "authentic leadership" model, leaders who genuinely listen to and incorporate follower's ideas into their leadership style, who are transparent in decision-making processes, and who remain true to a moral code engender trust and commitment from followers. These theories and others serve to remind us that it's the followers who actually get the job done, and leaders must genuinely care for their teammates, demonstrating that care by knowing them and putting their needs ahead of those of the leader.

THE DELICATE BALANCE: MISSION VS. PEOPLE

At the same time, we know that a focus on the mission is still required. Certainly, a leader who focuses so much on the mission that his or her followers either (at best) do no more than the minimum requirements or (at worst) abandon the team altogether will *not* be successful. And a leader who focuses so much on the followers, the "country club" model of leadership, that he or she is unable to accomplish the mission or task at hand will also fail. Extensive research has demonstrated that good leaders find a balance, focusing on both the mission and the welfare of their team simultaneously.

LEADERSHIP REQUIRES GOOD LEADERS AND GOOD FOLLOWERS

To go a step further, the most recent theories tell us that leadership is most successful when it's shared between leaders and followers. The actions required for good leadership (for example, planning, organizing, training, monitoring, challenging the team, finding resources, and solving problems) draw upon a significant number of skillsets. The diverse backgrounds, abilities, perspectives, and ideas brought together by a group of people *are the most important strengths of the group*. Researchers show that organizations that leverage these strengths by expecting leadership participation from *all members of the group* outperform those in which a single leader takes on all leadership roles. Maritime leaders, when placed in command, must *insist* on leadership from all members of the team; and when not placed in charge, they must contribute leadership to help the team be its best.

The preceding pages describe only a few of the many leadership approaches in order to instigate a lifelong study.

Every leader, whether a small-section leader of four individuals or the CEO of a Fortune 500 company, incorporates some of the styles described earlier. It is incumbent on all leaders to continually improve the understanding of their trade not only through their own personal experiences each day and building relationships with mentors but also with a general study of leadership. This includes consulting case studies, exploring different leadership approaches (such as those described in this chapter), and experimenting with new styles and techniques that can complement and potentially improve their personal style and abilities. One's leadership capability is not a static trait; it grows with each experience over time. Taking an active role in developing this capability through greater leadership education can transform a gradual growth into a radical transformation.

CHAPTER 3

LEADERSHIP DEFINED
THROUGH LISTS

⚓

> Officers and others in authority . . . are required
> to show in themselves a good example of virtue,
> honor, patriotism, and subordination.
>
> They will be vigilant in inspecting the con-
> duct of all persons; they will guard against
> and suppress dissolute and immoral practices
> according to regulations.
>
> They will take all necessary and proper
> measures under the laws, regulations, and cus-
> toms to promote and safeguard the moral, physi-
> cal well-being, and general welfare of the officers
> and enlisted personnel under their command.
>
> —*TITLE 10, U.S. CODE*

D efining leadership is both easy and hard. It's easy
because anyone can define it any way they want.
In this book, you'll see a hundred quotes from a
hundred great leaders, and they each have their own definition. And, in a sense, they're all right.

Yet defining proper leadership is hard: it not only is
complicated and nuanced but also depends on the situation,
the leader, and those being led. That's why on Amazon.com
there are over 40,000 books on leadership. And those are just
the ones available today.

> **Leadership is a process of persuasion and example, by which others are motivated to take action.**
> —*John Gardner* and *Ron Heifetz*

One thing is certain: any discussion of leadership is prone to produce lists.

What's the perfect house? Well, it depends. What is perfect for one person might be anathema for another. But if we're unable to "define" a perfect home, we can at least provide a list of home characteristics that most people find perfect in most situations, such as a fireplace, a modern kitchen, multiple bedrooms, large rooms, walk-in closets, a two-car garage, windows with a view, energy efficiency, and so on. Faced with something too difficult to describe exactly and universally, we search for a list of attributes.

Characteristics of a Boy Scout:			
Trustworthy	Friendly	Obedient	Brave
Loyal	Courteous	Cheerful	Clean
Helpful	Kind	Thrifty	Reverent

—*Boy Scout Handbook*

A hundred years ago, the Boy Scouts were trying to describe how to be a good scout, and solved the problem by listing the twelve attributes the organization expected of each member. So it is with leadership. We can't define it exactly because it means so many things to so many people under so many circumstances. But we can list attributes that great leaders seem to share. We can list skills that leaders seem to employ. We can list actions that leaders often take. We can list circumstances in which leadership has an effect. We can list triggers and sets of rules that seem to connect skill, action, and effect.

The great pointillist painters didn't paint in brush-strokes—they created tiny dots of paint that cumulatively created an expansive and perfectly understandable picture. Close up, all one sees is dots; from a distance, the image becomes clear. Defining leadership by lists seems to accomplish the same thing.

Leadership—it's hard to define. So embrace the lists and their utility!

SUMMARIZING THE LISTS

The premise to this primer on leadership is that you are too busy to spend hundreds of hours reading books on leadership. Your life is time constrained away from study: standing watch; leading your troops; tending to your ship, your aircraft, your people; and maybe catching some liberty (or some sleep) now and then. So we've selected from those forty thousand publications on Amazon about thirty-five books on leadership that might be most germane to the young leader in the sea services.

The next few pages squeeze the contents of those thirty-five books into several buckets of condensed thought. More precisely, they provide the "lists" of leadership traits, attributes, practices, rules, and concepts provided in those volumes. The ten thousand pages of wisdom in those thirty-five books don't represent the totality of all thought on leadership, obviously. But they're a pretty good start for a young leader like you.

Those titles come in three basic groups: books from the sea services, books from other services, and business/academic books. Together, they include hundreds of different leadership lists, many of which are provided to you in this chapter. A complete list of the thirty-five books is provided in appendix A.

The wisdom of the many leadership lists in those books seems to fall into three major groups:

A. Attributes and Traits of Leaders—what they seem to *be*

B. Competencies and Skills of Leaders—what they *do*

C. Models of Leadership—how one can *define* leadership as a process

Finally, the books sometimes provide straightforward advice: "do this, don't do that." Some of that is also provided in chapter 9. No one human is qualified to give you the definitive list of attributes of a leader. It doesn't exist. But by scanning the lists below from the thirty-five collective works of dozens of authors, representing hundreds of years of effort and wisdom, you can begin to see trends and commonalities that can inform your own definition of what leadership is.

So, read on through the lists and find the nuggets of truth that ring most true to you. Then you'll have your own personal definition of what leadership means.

GROUP A: THE ATTRIBUTES AND TRAITS OF A LEADER

As we've mentioned before, it's hard to say exactly what leadership is, but all authors on leadership seem to have their own list of the qualities, or the attributes, of a leader. In fact, eight of the thirty-five books contain a definitive "qualities of a leader" list.

Was there commonality or consensus between the eight lists? You bet. Of the eight, six include the following attributes as necessary qualities:

- Integrity and Character
- Endurance, Tenacity, Stamina, "Stick-to-it-iveness"

Five of the eight lists agree on the following attributes:

- Physical Courage
- Initiative
- Knowledge / Intelligence
- Maturity / Judgment
- Self-Discipline

Finally, four of the eight lists include the following common traits:

- Moral Courage
- Decisiveness
- Loyalty
- Enthusiasm / Optimism
- Selflessness
- Effective Communication (both speaking and writing)

This baker's dozen of attributes was common throughout the lists in these leadership books and appeared time and time again throughout all the other titles. If you're looking for a list of attributes you want to cultivate, consider the thirteen above. That's the summary. Now let's glance over some specifics. First, let's look at what books on Navy leadership have to say.

———————⚓———————

The Naval Officer's Guide, edited by CDR Lesa McComas, USN (Ret.), and CDR J. D. Kristenson, USN, covers all the nuances of being a naval officer. Chapter 18 covers leadership and lists the following twenty-one attributes or traits of the successful seagoing leader:

> I divide officers into four classes—the clever, the lazy, the stupid, and the industrious. Each officer possesses at least two of these qualities.
>
> —*Kurt von Hammerstein-Equord*

1. Knowledge
2. Integrity
3. Loyalty
4. Maturity
5. Will
6. Followership
7. Self-Discipline
8. Confidence
9. Flexibility
10. Endurance
11. Decisiveness
12. Initiative
13. Justice
14. Compassion
15. Forcefulness
16. Positive Attitude

17. Communication Skills
18. Foster Teamwork
19. Humility
20. Personal Behavior (ethical and moral)
21. Courage (physical and moral)

The textbook *Fundamentals of Naval Leadership,* edited by the legendary Naval Academy leadership professor Karel Montor, contains a similar list:

1. Integrity
2. Dependability
3. Cooperation
4. Loyalty
5. Unselfishness
6. Sense of Humor
7. Tact
8. Ability to Write Well
9. Ability to Speak Effectively
10. Initiative
11. Judgment
12. Enthusiasm
13. Creativity
14. Decisiveness
15. Endurance
16. Self-Discipline
17. Moral Courage
18. Physical Courage

⚓

Professor Montor and his team interviewed dozens of senior naval officers to produce another textbook, *Naval*

Leadership: Voices of Experience. In it, there are four different lists of attributes worth noting.

The Basis of Leadership	Other Requirements for Leadership
Personal Example	Physical Stamina
Moral Responsibility	Mental Stamina
Good Management	Putting Others before Self
Tact	Working Harder than Subordinates
Dependability	Objectivity
Sense of Humor	Accountability

Components of Professionalism	Characteristics of an Officer
Integrity	Judgment
Pride	Imagination
Expertise	Analytical Ability
Loyalty to Country	Impeccable Personal Behavior
Pleasure in Work	Military Bearing
Self Improvement	Forcefulness
Selecting and Utilizing Subordinates	Speaking and Writing Ability
Self-Discipline	Self-Improvement
	Correcting Perceived Wrongs

Montor, K., ed. 1998. *Naval Leadership: Voices of Experience.* 2nd ed. Annapolis, MD: Naval Institute Press.

Finally, among naval texts, *Command at Sea,* a guidebook for commanding officers written by ADM James Stavridis, identifies eight "distinctly American" naval leadership traditions that have applied to American ship captains over the ages:

1. Use of Initiative
2. Boldness and Daring
3. Tenacity
4. Courage

5. Assertiveness
6. Ingenuity
7. Initiative of Juniors
8. Decision Making

⚓

What about traits and attributes identified from other services besides the Navy?

ADM James Loy, USCG, in the excellent text *Character in Action: The U.S. Coast Guard on Leadership*, writes that one should look for seven qualities in the people a leader chooses to be around. They are:

1. Intelligence
2. High Energy
3. Self-Confidence
4. Continual Learning
5. Compassion
6. Courage with a Bias toward Action
7. Character

⚓

The *U.S. Army Leadership Field Manual* lists the following attributes of a leader:

1. Will
2. Self-Discipline
3. Initiative
4. Judgment
5. Self-Confidence
6. Cultural Awareness
7. Intelligence

8. Health and Physical Fitness
9. Military and Professional Bearing
10. Self-Control
11. Balance
12. Stability

⚓

The Armed Forces Officer lists the following attributes expected of an American leader:

Honor: The compelling moral motivation to do the right thing at the right time.

Respect: The positive regard one person evidences for the shared humanity of another.

Duty: A moral obligation to place accomplishment of the assigned task before all personal needs and apprehensions.

Service: The officer is the servant of the nation. Service entails dedicating one's very life to something higher and more important than one's own gratification.

Excellence: A deep-seated personal passion for continuous improvement, innovation, and exemplary results in all endeavors.

Courage: The will to act rightly in the face of physical, personal, or professional danger or adversity.

Commitment: Total dedication to success.

Loyalty: A true, willing, and unfailing devotion to a cause.

Integrity: The willingness to do what is right even when no one is looking. An unwavering moral compass.

Another great list from the Army comes from GEN George Patton in *Patton on Leadership*. The general's personal list of the "chief qualities of leadership" is as follows:

1. Perfection of detail (being able to pay attention to the little things)
2. Personal supervision
3. Thorough and detailed knowledge of the business at hand
4. A strong physical leadership presence
5. The ability to set a personal example
6. The ability to communicate, to explain orders
7. The commitment to ensure that orders are correctly executed

On a more current, less military note, *Leadership for Dummies* has a somewhat different viewpoint in its "Ten Characteristics of a True Leader":

1. Eagerness
2. Cheerfulness
3. Honesty
4. Resourcefulness
5. Persuasiveness
6. Cooperation
7. Altruism
8. Courage
9. Supportiveness
10. Assertiveness

Notice how we've seen some traits before, including honesty, courage, and assertiveness. But others provide a different perspective: eagerness, altruism? Once again, leadership looks different to different viewers.

Rather than rely on an individual's view of what constitutes leadership, the college postgraduate leadership textbook *The Nature of Leadership* identifies a list of approximately twenty "Key Attributes" of a leader, as determined by empirical studies over the last twenty years. These attributes fall into seven primary buckets:

1. Cognitive Capacities
   - General intelligence
   - Creative thinking
2. Personality
   - Extroversion
   - Conscientiousness
   - Emotional stability
   - Openness
   - Agreeableness
   - Tested preferences for extroversion, intuition, thinking, and judging
3. Motives and Needs
   - Need for power
   - Need for achievement
   - Motivation to lead
4. Social Capacities
   - Self-monitoring
   - Social intelligence
5. Emotional intelligence

6. Problem-Solving Skills
   - Problem construction
   - Solution generation
   - Metacognition
7. Tacit Knowledge

⚓

One of our favorite leadership lists comes from the well-written and aptly named business book *The 21 Indispensable Qualities of a Leader,* by John C. Maxwell. The list is provided here in its entirety:

1. Character: Be a Piece of the Rock
2. Charisma: The First Impression Can Seal the Deal
3. Commitment: It Separates Doers from Dreamers
4. Communication: Without It You Travel Alone
5. Competence: If You Build It, They Will Come
6. Courage: One Person with Courage Is a Majority
7. Discernment: Put an End to Unsolved Mysteries
8. Focus: The Sharper It Is, the Sharper You Are
9. Generosity: Your Candle Loses Nothing When It Lights Another
10. Initiative: You Won't Leave Home without It
11. Listening: To Connect with Their Hearts, Use Your Ears
12. Passion: Take This Life and Love It
13. Positive Attitude: If You Believe You Can, You Can
14. Problem Solving: You Can't Let Your Problems Be a Problem
15. Relationships: If You Get Along, They'll Go Along

16. Responsibility: If You Won't Carry the Ball, You Can't Lead the Team
17. Security: Competence Never Compensates for Insecurity
18. Self-Discipline: The First Person You Lead Is You
19. Servanthood: To Get Ahead, Put Others First
20. Teachability: To Keep Leading, Keep Learning
21. Vision: You Can Seize Only What You Can See

Although Maxwell's book is targeted primarily for the business market (with over a million copies sold to date), notice how the leadership traits listed are so similar to the traits listed previously for military leaders.

Finally, no list on leadership traits could be complete without a reference to arguably the greatest leader of the twentieth century, Winston Churchill. In *Churchill on Leadership*, Sir Winston's personal leadership traits are as follows:

- Courage and Optimism
- Kindness, Magnanimity, and Gratitude
- Independent Judgment and Self-Criticism
- Loyalty to the Team
- Rest, Relaxation, and Change of Pace
- Calmness under Stress
- Personal Contact with Subordinates
- Ability to Face Bad News Squarely and Candidly

As you can see, there are many ways of looking at leadership traits and characteristics. None are exactly the same, but there are enough commonalities to give you a clear picture of what a real leader should be. In chapter 10, as you build your own leadership development plan, we'll ask you to list what you think are the traits *you* view as necessary for a leader. But before then, let's move past leadership traits (what they *are*), and move on to what leaders *do*—their competencies.

GROUP B: THE COMPETENCIES AND SKILLS OF A LEADER

Remember, we're summarizing thirty-five leadership books, representing ten thousand pages and hundreds of lists about leadership. In the previous section, we reviewed what those books provided as the traits of leadership. But they also describe leadership in terms of competencies—that's what we'll look at now.

As we've done before, let's look at the seagoing viewpoint first, then the view of other military services, and finally the view from business and academia. In the textbook *Fundamentals of Naval Leadership,* produced by the Department of Leadership, Ethics, and Law at the Naval Academy, the following list of leadership competencies is provided. According to the text, an effective leader

- sets the example
- has learned to be a good follower
- knows her job
- establishes objectives and plans for their accomplishment
- knows himself and seeks self-improvement
- takes responsibility for her actions, regardless of their outcome

- is consistent, but not inflexible
- seeks responsibility
- develops a sense of responsibility among his subordinates
- treats every person as an individual, not a number
- keeps his subordinates informed
- encourages subordinates to offer suggestions and/or constructive criticism
- makes sure the task is understood, supervised, and accomplished
- trains her subordinates as a team
- employs the unit in accordance with its capabilities

The Division Officer's Guide could be described as a handbook for junior officers and petty officers in the U.S. Navy and the U.S. Coast Guard. Coauthored by ADM James Stavridis, it's a great book for any young seagoing officer. It lists five primary leadership competencies for the aspiring leader:

- Communication
- Supervision
- Teaching and counseling
- Team development
- Personal competencies

The sage senior officers in *Naval Leadership: Voices of Experience* collectively view eight major steps necessary to accomplish a mission. The required competencies for any officer who wants to be effective are:

> Hereafter, if you should observe an occasion to give your
> officers and friends a little more praise than is their due, and
> confess more fault than you can justly be charged with, you
> will only become the sooner for it, a great captain.
>
> —Benjamin Franklin in a letter to John Paul Jones

1. Know the Job
2. Plan the Mission
3. Implement the Plan
4. Monitor Progress
5. Motivate
6. Maintain Morale
7. Make Things Happen through People
8. Provide Training

⚓

The Department of Defense, through the National Defense University Press, publishes *The Armed Forces Officer,* which describes the following five leadership competencies:

1. Leadership is a bond of trust.
2. Leaders set and enforce the standards.
3. Leaders set the example.
4. Leaders model courage, both physical and moral.
5. Leaders build and sustain morale.

⚓

Charles Garcia graduated from the Air Force Academy and served as an officer before being selected for the prestigious White House Fellows program. He studied White House fellows and the leaders they worked for, which resulted in the book *Leadership Lessons of the White House Fellows*. Garcia devotes a chapter to each of twenty primary leadership competencies:

1. Leaders know there's more to life than work.
2. Leaders focus on the mission.
3. Leaders have a laserlike focus on their people.
4. Leaders root out prejudice in themselves and others.
5. Leaders act with integrity.
6. Leaders create a sense of urgency.
7. Leaders have passion.
8. Leaders are persistent.
9. Leaders are great communicators.
10. Leaders ask the tough questions that need to be asked.
11. Leaders take risks.
12. Leaders understand that not every battle is the end of the war.
13. Leaders energize their people.
14. Leaders are great listeners.
15. Leaders are persuasive.
16. Leaders know when to compromise and when to stand firm.
17. Leaders are problem solvers.
18. Leaders lead by walking around.
19. Leaders are transformational change agents.
20. Leaders lead through experience and competence, not through title or position.

The civilians of the Department of Homeland Security (DHS) are led by members of the Senior Executive Service (SES). Those in the SES are equivalent in rank to generals and admirals among federal government workers. DHS has defined eight "Core Leadership Competencies" that it wants these federal leaders to demonstrate, and each SES member is rated each year against these requirements. It's a fabulous description of senior leadership in a complex organization. DHS wants each of its leaders to be

1. Principled—adheres to the highest ethical standards of public service and integrity
2. People Centered—engages, values, motivates, mentors, recruits, clearly directs, and appropriately rewards employees
3. Effective Communicator—defines the mission with clarity; listens effectively; shares information
4. Performance Centered—establishes and meets clear and meaningful goals; uses good judgment in decision making
5. A Diversity Advocate—promotes workforce diversity; provides equitable recognition and equal opportunity; addresses allegations of harassment or discrimination
6. Highly Collaborative—partners effectively within and across DHS components and with external local, state, and international partners
7. Nimble and Innovative—brings creative discipline to encourage continuous innovation

8. A Steward of Public Resources—ensures financial and managerial accountability; takes care of financial and information resources

On a more business-oriented note, Personnel Decisions International Corporation publishes the *Successful Executive's Handbook,* which identifies twenty-two specific leadership skillsets grouped into eight primary competencies.

1. Thinking
   - Reasoned Judgment
   - Visionary Thinking
   - Financial Acumen
   - Global Perspective
2. Strategic Management
   - Shaping Strategy
   - Driving Execution
3. Leadership
   - Attracting and Developing Talent
   - Empowering Others
   - Influencing and Negotiating
   - Leadership Versatility
4. Interpersonal
   - Building Organizational Relationships
   - Inspiring Trust
5. Communication
   - High-Impact Delivery
   - Fostering Open Dialogue
6. Motivation
   - Entrepreneurial Risk Taking
   - Drive for Stakeholder Success

  7. Self-Management
      • Career and Self-Direction
      • Adaptability
      • Mature Confidence
  8. Breadth and Depth
      • Business-Situation Versatility
      • Industry Knowledge
      • Cross-Functional Capability

Similarly, the American Management Association publishes the *AMA Handbook of Leadership*. In the chapter
"What Is an Effective Leader?" the authors list five rules
and four overarching competencies for leaders.

The five rules are as follows:

  1. Shape the future. Leaders must strategize the
     future they intend to create.
  2. Make things happen. Leaders must execute.
  3. Engage today's talent. Leaders must build strong
     teams.
  4. Build the next generation. Leaders must develop
     today's human capital into tomorrow's team
     leaders.
  5. Invest in yourself. Leaders must learn their job
     and their craft as a leader.

The four general observations on competencies:

  1. All leaders must excel at personal proficiency.
  2. All leaders must have one towering strength.

3. Each leader must be at least average in his or her "weaker" leadership domains.
4. Leaders must be able to grow.

⚓

Speaking of business books, you've no doubt seen the plethora of publications that begin with "Leadership Lessons of [Famous Name]," or "[Famous Name] on Leadership." The "famous names" include Gandhi, John Wooden, John F. Kennedy, Shakespeare, Anthony Zinni, Irwin Rommel, fictional character Tony Soprano, Moses, Robert E. Lee, Churchill, Patton, Attila the Hun, Lincoln, and on and on. One of the books of this genre is *The Leadership Lessons of Jesus*. It includes the following list of leadership competencies:

1. Leaders call followers.
2. Leaders teach with authority.
3. Leaders take care of their people.
4. Leadership requires discipline.
5. Leaders expect the unexpected.
6. Leaders eat with the troops.
7. Leaders use traditions.
8. Leaders plan.
9. Leaders tell stories.
10. Leaders are faithful.
11. Leaders are visible.
12. Leaders take decisive action.

⚓

On a more academic note, the postgraduate textbook *The Nature of Leadership* provides two excellent lists of leadership skills, basic and advanced, based on an overview of academic literature on the subject. These may be the most comprehensive and useful lists available. Use them to measure yourself in chapter 10!

Basic Leadership Skills	Advanced Leadership Skills
Learning from Experience	Delegating
Communication	Managing Conflict
Listening	Negotiation
Assertiveness	Problem Solving
Providing Constructive Feedback	Improving Creativity
Effective Stress Management	Diagnosing Performance Problems
Technical Competence	Team Building
Effective Relationships with Superiors	Building High Performance Teams
Effective Relationships with Peers	Development Planning
Setting Goals	Credibility
Punishment	Coaching
Conducting Meetings	Empowerment

So, do you have a sense of the ten or fifteen *traits* that you want to imbue in yourself as a leader? Do you have another dozen *competencies and skills* you feel you need to develop? Great! In chapter 9, we'll look at a new set of lists—lists of advice from older, wiser writers to young, budding leaders like yourself. But first, let's look at some ways in which others have combined traits with competencies and skills to produce an idea of what leadership looks like.

GROUP C: THE MODELS OF LEADERSHIP

We began this chapter by stating that leadership is hard to define but that attempts to define it often result in lists. We've seen lists of traits (who the leader is) and competencies and skills (what the leader does). Now let's look at one final way of defining leadership: models.

Models incorporate not only traits and skills but also situations and advice. They attempt to provide a single construct in which one can define and understand the complex process of leadership. Let's look at the different leadership models hidden within the ten thousand pages of those thirty-five books, starting with two very useful models from the Coast Guard.

The commandant of the Coast Guard issued "Commandant Instruction M5351.3: Leadership Development Framework" in May 2006. It's constructed around the Coast Guard's twenty-eight leadership competencies, which are organized into four primary groups. Notice how each group builds upon its predecessor; the leader starts with leading self, then leading others, then leading organizations.

1. Leading Self
   - Accountability and Responsibility
   - Followership
   - Self-Awareness and Learning
   - Aligning Values
   - Health and Well-Being
   - Personal Conduct
   - Technical Proficiency

2. Leading Others
   - Effective Communications
   - Influencing Others
   - Respect for Others and Diversity Management
   - Team Building
   - Taking Care of People
   - Mentoring

3. Leading Performance and Change
   - Customer Focus
   - Management and Process Improvement
   - Decision Making and Problem Solving
   - Conflict Management
   - Creativity and Innovation
   - Vision Development and Implementation

4. Leading the Coast Guard
   - Stewardship
   - Technology Management
   - Financial Management
   - Human Resource Management
   - Partnering
   - External Awareness
   - Entrepreneurship
   - Political Savvy
   - Strategic Thinking

⚓

Another leadership model is provided in *Character in Action: The U.S. Coast Guard on Leadership*. In it, authors Donald Phillips and ADM James Loy lay out an excellent plan for developing as a leader.

1. Set the Foundation
   - Define the Culture and Live the Values
   - Select the Best
   - Promote Team over Self
   - Instill a Commitment to Excellence

2. Focus on People
   - Eliminate the Frozen Middle (cut middle management opposed to change)
   - Cultivate Caring Relationships
   - Build Strong Alliances
   - Create an Effective Communication System

Progress always involves risks. You can't steal second base and keep your foot on first.

—*Frederick B. Wilcox*

---

3. Instill a Bias for Action
   - Make Change the Norm
   - Encourage Decisiveness
   - Empower the Young
   - Give Priority to Those in the Field

4. Ensure the Future
   - Leverage Resources
   - Sponsor Continual Learning
   - Spotlight Excellence
   - Honor History and Tradition

⚓

VADM James Stockdale provides an entirely different model for leadership. In *Ethics and the Military Profession:*

Moral Foundations of Leadership, contributor Col Paul Rousch, USMC, writes about Stockdale's model for "Value- and Principle-Centered Leadership." As you'll recall, Stockdale was awarded the Medal of Honor as a POW in Vietnam, was later president of the Naval War College and the Citadel, and was Ross Perot's vice-presidential running mate in the 1992 presidential election.

> *"The Stockdale Leadership Model: Value- and Principle-Centered Leadership"*
>
> *Leaders are imbued with national and professional values.*
> *   –Their reference points are the Constitution and their services' core values.*
> *   –They incorporate these values into five leadership roles:*
> *   –Moralist, Teacher, Jurist, Steward, and Philosopher*
>
> *Leaders in the role of MORALIST make plain the good by the way they live their lives.*
> *   –Leaders are people of honor.*
> *   –Leaders demonstrate a disciplined lifestyle for emulation by their followers.*
> *   –Leaders exercise a priority of loyalties.*
>
> *Leaders in the role of JURIST make decisions, rules, and policies based on the strength of their character.*
> *   –Leaders hold themselves accountable for all their units do or fail to do.*
> *   –Leaders enhance their followers' ability to know what is right and do what is right.*
> *   –Leaders act upon well-placed conviction.*

Leaders in the role of TEACHER provide a sense of perspective and set the moral, social, and particularly the motivational climate in a unit.

> *–Leaders appeal to their followers' highest aspirations.*
> *–Leaders create confidence in their followers by serving as the catalyst for decisive, forceful action when appropriate.*
> *–Leaders create a climate which promotes unit cohesion.*
> *–Leaders enhance unit effectiveness.*

Leaders in the role of STEWARD invest their lives in the lives of their followers.

> *–Leaders view themselves as servants.*
> *–Leaders guard the fundamental dignity of their followers.*
> *–Leaders understand human nature and value individual differences.*

Leaders in the role of PHILOSOPHER persevere "when virtue is not rewarded and evil is not punished."

> *–Leaders do their duty because it is their duty.*
> *–Leaders know how to deal with uncertainty and adapt to change.*

⚓

Yet another very different model is provided by the Army in the *U.S. Army Leadership Field Manual.* We like it because it's simple, understandable, and memorable. It also seems to fit well with the preponderance of leadership discussions in the thirty-five books we're reviewing.

The model is "Be, Know, Do."

Be consists of Values and Attributes.

> *Values include Loyalty, Duty, Respect, Selfless Service, Honor, Integrity, and Courage.*
>
> *Attributes include Mental, Physical, and Emotional traits.*

Know consists of Skills: Interpersonal, Conceptual, Technical, and Tactical.

Do consists of Influencing, Operating, and Improving.

> *Influencing means Communicating, Decision Making, and Motivating.*
>
> *Operating means Planning, Preparing, Executing, and Assessing.*
>
> *Improving means Developing, Building, and Learning.*

⚓

Since shortly after 9/11, the Coast Guard has been a component within the Department of Homeland Security (DHS). Within that service's official "Instruction on Leadership" is the DHS's five-step model for leadership competence. Like the Coast Guard model shown previously, this one builds step by step, with each step requiring competence in its predecessor first. This model is broad enough to make sense in virtually all organizations, both military and civilian.

1. Core Competencies (All employees, including junior newcomers)
   - Communication
   - Influencing/Negotiating
   - Customer Service
   - Resilience
   - Interpersonal Skills
   - Continual Learning
   - Flexibility
   - Integrity/Honesty

2. Team/Project Leader
   - Team Building
   - Technical Credibility
   - Problem Solving
   - Accountability
   - Decisiveness

3. Supervisor
   - Human Resource Management
   - Leveraging Diversity
   - Conflict Management
   - Service Motivation

4. Manager
   - Technology Management
   - Financial Management
   - Creativity and Innovation
   - Partners

5. Executive
   - External Awareness
   - Vision

- Strategic Thinking
- Entrepreneurship
- Political Savvy

⚓

LESSONS FROM THE LISTS

What lessons can we draw from all this? In this chapter, we've just skimmed over the wave tops of thirty-five books written by dozens of authors, comprising some ten thousand pages of leadership advice. What does it all mean?

It means that leadership can be described in many different ways. There is no one leadership way, nor only one way to describe leadership. But we can still draw lessons from the lists. For instance, if we analyze the lists themselves, the following twenty-seven leadership words appear most frequently:

Most Common Leadership Words from Thirty-Five Books on Leadership		
know	moral	physical
make	skills	commitment
self	responsibility	development
people	focus	honor
service	vision	followers
team	create	example
effective	press	decisions
courage	build	trust
others	lessons	plan

Courage. Responsibility. Vision. Commitment. Service. Notice how those words appear in many of the books on leadership—and likely in other books you've read on the subject.

And, if you look closely at the lists, you'll see six common themes:

- Knowing your job.
- Taking care of your people.
- Delegation and follow up.
- Loyalty to the team and the cause.
- Being an honorable person of character.
- Setting goals and helping others achieve.

In other words, while a thousand people will paint their picture of leadership in a thousand different ways, they'll use only a dozen or so brushstrokes and just a few colors. There are commonalities.

I find the great thing in this world is not so much where we stand, as in what direction we are moving. To reach a point we must sail, sometimes with the wind, and sometimes against it. But we must not drift or lie at anchor.

—*Oliver Wendell Holmes*

For chapter 9, we interviewed 380 senior officers from the sea services and asked them for *their* definition of leadership in the young seagoing leader. These men and women represent nine thousand years of cumulative service. And it's extraordinary how close their collective definition of leadership meets the six themes listed above.

Your job, before this book is over, is to find what *your* portrait of leadership looks like.

But before we do that, over the next five chapters, let's examine dozens of lessons from experienced sea-service leaders. Hopefully, as you read their sea stories, you'll recognize the six themes above and the attributes and skills that have appeared in the leadership lists presented in this chapter.

CHAPTER 4

JUNIOR OFFICER
LEADERSHIP LESSONS

The foundation of leadership is character.
—*GEN ALEXANDER PATCH*

You don't manage people; you manage things.
You lead people.

—*RADM GRACE HOPPER*

I have found that being honest is the best technique I can use. Right up front, tell people what you're trying to accomplish and what you're willing to sacrifice to accomplish it.

—*LEE IACOCCA*

Leaders don't just hold sailors accountable, they are responsible for developing accountable sailors.
—*VADM JOHN B. MUSTIN*

It's important that people know what you stand for. It's equally important that they know what you won't stand for.

—*MARY WALDROP*

There is a great deal of talk about loyalty from the bottom to the top. Loyalty from the top down is even more necessary and much less prevalent.
—*GEN GEORGE S. PATTON*

I n addition to exposing you to the principles of sound leadership and to sharing those personal, ethical, motivational, and professional attributes we've found consistently rooted within historically successful leaders, we also recognize the value of sharing relevant *lessons learned*. In this chapter, our intent is to share anecdotes that communicate specific lessons you can learn from *today*, regardless of your service, community, or experience level, because they have obvious implications for things you are likely to see while operating afloat. Of course, there are unique differences between operating on a submarine, on a destroyer, on a merchant vessel, or on land, but the lessons we share offer leadership lessons of a timeless platform- and service-agnostic basis so you can learn from others' experiences. Enjoy the following accounts!

FIXING IT RIGHT

When I checked on board my ship for my second tour, I was at 55-percent manning, without a chief petty officer, without a first class petty officer, and six days out from the ship's first forward-deployed patrol out of Rota, Spain. I was in over my head. However, I quickly realized that who I had on my team was more important than how many people I had on my team. I relied immensely on a team of my hardest-working and brightest Sailors, as well as support from the department, in order to keep our heads above water.

The hours were long and the work was hard. Thankfully, we returned home safely four months later, just in time to meet our new chief on the pier and begin preparations for a year-long inspection-and-certification cycle.

As the first portion of our inspection came up, we knew that it was extremely important that we perform well. As a forward-deployed warship, there was not much room for error; and I knew that if we failed the inspection, we would impact our ability to deploy and thus our ability to meet our mission. The pressure was on.

As fate would have it, my team discovered a significant discrepancy the week the inspectors were due to arrive. There was no way we would be able to legitimately correct the issue in the time we had. However, there were several ways we could have "gotten the job done" and passed the inspection, of course, with the intent to permanently fix the issue at a later date. This was tempting; especially as I imagined the conversation I would have with the captain telling him we wouldn't be able to pass the inspection.

My same team that pulled us through that first deployment, plus my new hard-charging chief, put their heads together to come up with a better plan. Instead of covering up our error, we turned to fix it as best we could. I briefed my boss and my captain on the discrepancy, its impact, as well as our plan to fix it. While it was not a pleasant conversation, I learned several things from the interaction.

Most importantly, I solidified my captain's trust in me, as well as my Sailors. When the inspectors arrived, I explained our situation and the way forward—and to my surprise, they were impressed by our hard work and, more importantly, our integrity. The trust between the inspectors and my division was established that day and would prove to be essential throughout the duration of the inspection. My takeaway was that the culture that was set in our division during this experience valued productive teamwork, was rooted in integrity, and carried us through the deployments to come.

—*LT Marina Nanartowich, USN*

PRAISE IN PUBLIC

One of the enduring principles of leadership is that you praise in public and criticize or rebuke in private. As the following sea story illustrates, failure to adhere to this principle can have unintended consequences. I reported as a chief engineer (CHENG) just prior to the first deployment of my ship. That deployment went exceptionally well, the ship earned a very positive reputation, and the captain, who had joined the ship en route to WestPac, was highly regarded by the crew (an important point for the purpose of this story). In late summer of that year, the ship was assigned as part of a carrier screen during a deployment to the Mediterranean. Somewhere about mid-Atlantic on a sunny morning with an extremely tranquil sea, a leak developed in a flange of the high-pressure steam line going to the main engine. The flange was located just outside the main-control portside door, where it posed a very serious safety hazard to personnel. The captain was duly notified, who then notified the admiral of the problem and that we were going to have to go dead in the water (DIW). The unrealistic hope and plan as conveyed to the admiral was that we would let the system cool down for 60–90 minutes and then torque the flange bolts in hopes that the leak would stop. This plan was carried out, we started to build steam to the engine, but the flange still leaked. We dutifully notified the admiral of this and that we had no alternative but to go DIW again and let the system cool down enough so that we could replace the flange seal without risking warping of the new seal (only one replacement was carried). We gave the admiral an estimate of six hours without really having any idea of what the time would really be.

During this repair time, the carrier and its screen circled us. It was definitely not the kind of visibility that the crew of a ship wants regardless of rank or rate. After about four hours, we decided to attempt the replacement. That process was relatively fast, after which we began to slowly elevate the flange temperature. After an elapsed time of about four-and-a-half hours, we notified the bridge that we were ready to answer all bells. With that, the captain ordered me via the squawk box to report to the bridge. I reported to the bridge fully expecting a dressing down but also expecting that the captain would ask me to follow him to his stateroom. Instead, in front of the bridge watch, he began to give me a profanity-laced tongue-lashing that was worse than I could have imagined. He screamed that I had embarrassed him, the ship, and the crew before the task group and made us the laughing stock of the Navy. For the better part of what seemed like five minutes, he hurled profanity-laced invectives at me and, by extension, my engineers. During the whole episode, the bridge-watch team had the most uncomfortable look on their faces. You could tell that everyone just wanted to evaporate.

There is no telling how long the captain's tirade might have gone on, but it was interrupted by the admiral calling the captain over the primary tactical circuit, which happened to be patched to the speaker on the bridge. The admiral proceeded to tell the captain (and everyone on the bridge) that he wanted his verbal commendation passed along to the engineers for doing in four-and-a-half hours what the carrier's CHENG had said would take six to seven hours. The admiral's call, which probably lasted about a minute, was nothing short of effusive in its praise. After the admiral signed off, you could hear a pin drop. The captain said nothing, getting out of his chair in a glaring rage and departing for his stateroom. After his departure, the bridge watch offered me its congratulations, and by mealtime, the bridge "scene" was a legend on the mess deck. The point of this story is that the captain destroyed in five minutes the esteem that he had earned from the crew in the previous year. He never regained that esteem, all because he forgot the principle of praise in public, rebuke in private.

—*LCDR Jeffrey Belden, USN, CHENG*

START TOUGH, THEN BACK OFF

When I was a new ensign, I was sent to my first ship and was assigned a division. When I arrived, my division was a mess. They didn't have a chief petty officer in charge, and the division suffered from a lack of discipline and leadership. I came in as the nice-guy officer who tried to lead through example, and through consensus, and through discussing things with the group. The division soon branded me as a patsy, and despite my best efforts to cajole them into better performance, nothing much happened. They were known as the "dirt-bag" division.

Halfway through my first deployment with this gang, a chief petty officer was finally assigned to us. He flew in during a port call and spent the first couple of days on board in the Chiefs' Mess, getting the scoop on me and each member of the division. To this day, thirty years later, I still remember the first time we met him as we stood out at quarters on the flight deck, underway, in cold weather. I shook his hand and introduced him to the division. He promptly launched into a tirade about what a mess we were. He yelled. He stomped. He inspected each member of the division and spat out corrections on hair, uniform, shoes, posture, insignia. He announced out loud every bad thing he had heard from the Chiefs' Mess about each one of us. Frankly, he scared me to death, and I was technically his boss. I could see the sailors in the division stiffen with fear—a new sheriff was clearly in town, and boy, was he frightening!

For the next forty-eight hours or so, the new chief ran the division ragged. All new haircuts. Shined shoes. Lengthy lectures at quarters. Pressed uniforms. Corrections to watch standing. Seabag inspections. Berthing cleanups. No TV or movies—just work. He scared everyone in the division and worked them like they had never been worked before. I stayed away as much as I could.

And after forty-eight hours, it stopped, like the calm after a storm has passed through. The chief became his normal self—a mild, humorous, gentle man. For his next three years on board, I never again saw him get angry or raise his voice. But the division had gotten the message—they saw what he could be, and that was enough. From that day forward, they marched to his drummer—they met his standards—they obeyed him without question. Most importantly, the division became measurably better in every way.

The lesson I learned is that when a new boss starts off gentle and conciliatory, some may interpret it as weakness; it's hard to become the tough guy. I learned that it's better to start as the tough guy to set the standards high, and then back off.

—*RADM Robert Wray, USN (Ret.)*

KEEP YOUR BOSS INFORMED

Once as a young main-propulsion assistant (MPA) ensign on a destroyer, the commanding officer (CO) climbed down into my engine room around 0500 just after we threw a thrust bearing on the main shaft. When he asked, "How's it going?" I filled him in on the casualty. But now I had a significant problem: the CO knew about a major casualty but my boss, the CHENG, did not. The CO's shoes were not even out of sight as I was calling the CHENG in his stateroom. He was not pleased to get a phone call at 0515 and definitely not pleased to learn about the thrust bearing. I learned later that no sooner had he hung up his phone when the CO called him, asking "How's it going?" The CHENG was able to respond with information about the casualty, looking good to his boss.

The moral of the story is to keep your chain of command informed, especially when the chain gets jumped unexpectedly. I was so impressed with this lesson that it is to this day one of my guiding principles.

—*LT David Wyatt, USN*

LEADERSHIP IS LEADERSHIP

My first afloat leadership role was as a division officer for two engineering divisions on a nearly thirty-year-old, Norfolk-based amphibious helicopter carrier. While my two divisions were highly regarded in terms of the volume and the quality of the work they performed, they were notorious for the trouble they would get into, both on and off the ship. In the first month, these incidents ran the gamut from thefts to fighting. Supporting me in leading these two divisions was a broken-down chief petty officer who had no "gas in the tank," and who spent nearly all of his workday in the Chief's Mess. It was obvious to me that this chief either did not want to exert, or was incapable of exerting, any positive influence on the division. I brought it to the chief's attention in a counseling session, and I saw an initial improvement for about a week before things reverted to the prior norm.

Then I brought it to the command master chief (CMC), who thought that there was very little that could be done as the chief was little more than a year from retirement. I did not have that much time to wait for a new khaki leader, nor did I have the patience. I gave my department head and the CMC a heads-up that I was going to make a change that might make some waves. I pulled the chief out of the Chiefs' Mess one day and told him that he was no longer needed and that he could remain in the mess for the remaining time that he had onboard. I then pulled my first class petty officer aside one day after quarters and told him that he would be running the two divisions effective immediately. He initially asked about the chief, and I told him that the chief would no longer be running the divisions; that I was providing him the reins and the authority to lead. Then I walked him through my expectations and, at the same time, talked him through what success should look like. He was initially nervous about the responsibility, but when I explained to him that I would support him as long as he attacked the role aggressively and confidently, he was completely on board. I announced his role at the next quarters and left him with the sailors to frame his direction without my presence or involvement.

He proceeded to take the ball and run with it. He did such a good job over the next year that the ship made him a nominee for the extremely competitive Camp David Award, a recognition for which he was ultimately selected. The key takeaways for me was that leadership can come from many places—don't be afraid to make a move because you're concerned about ruffling some feathers. If your intentions are good, then folks will see that.

—*RDML Kevin Hayes, USN*

LEADERS: THE PROBLEM STARTS WITH YOU

I was sure I was about to be relieved.

As a young lieutenant commander, I'd recently taken command of an expeditionary patrol boat unit with a hard-earned reputation for being "operators." They had made two deployments in the two years prior to my arrival, and we were deep in predeployment workups for a third deployment in as many years. In short, they were seasoned, experienced experts in the missions, functions, and tasks that units like ours would be expected to perform.

My predecessor was well seasoned, having enjoyed several prior tours in the community, experience in Vietnam, and was a Mustang. By contrast, I was a new guy in this particular community, viewed skeptically as an Aegis, air-warfare, CRUDES, Academy guy coming into the expeditionary warfare community, the "Green Team."

My newcomer status afforded me the freedom to ask many questions—a technique I enjoyed both to learn but also to demonstrate to the team that I welcomed a questioning attitude. I wanted to reinforce that there was no monopoly of good ideas based on rank, rate, or experience—that we were all one team. And yet, over time, I learned my questions created a sense of uneasiness because some of the seasoned petty officers and chiefs—who weren't used to being questioned—felt I didn't trust them. My practice of delegating decision making to the lowest appropriate level created an immense culture shock given the prior CO's centralized control.

We were working on many things simultaneously, some of which were new to the Navy, most of which were new to me. All were urgent and important. I was asking lots of questions, but, in retrospect, I often failed to ask the *right* questions, or to probe beyond first contact when things didn't sound quite right. We were excellent operators, but commitments fell through the cracks, we experienced a towing casualty (thankfully without any injuries), and in a few cases, we made poor decisions about maintenance, with disastrous consequences. As CO, I recognized that the cumulative impact of these incidents didn't bode well for me, or my team.

Back to the call with the commodore. Luckily for me, this call did not result in my relief, though it was certainly stern (and memorable). When I hung up, I knew we needed to change how we did business.

My ah-ha moment was the realization that I needed to view outcomes over effort and consider delegation and accountability differently. Specifically, I changed my perspective in all things to acknowledge that "the problem started with me." If we failed, it wasn't a problem for my executive officer, a department head, or a chief—it was a failure for me. And I don't like failure.

Despite my slow start, our unit was remarkable, and we hit our stride in my second year. We lived through a cultural transformation, and the team delivered excellence daily, at home and in a combat theater. Our deployment was safe, professional, and operationally flawless—and to this day we enjoy a remarkable alumni network of talented Sailors and officers who continue to lead at the highest levels of the Navy.

A few of the key leadership lessons learned include:

- Communicate your vision and the reasons for the decisions you make. It's hard for a leader to "over-communicate."
- Leaders are not expected to come up with every idea. The responsibility of leadership is to establish a vision—an environment in which great ideas can thrive—and empower the team to figure out how to deliver it.
- Leaders create the conditions for teams to succeed and to hold those teams accountable for delivering. And they hold themselves accountable for team outcomes.

- Leaders should not strive to be the smartest person in the room, but rather to assemble and empower the best *team*.

—*VADM John B. Mustin, USN*

BREAKING DOWN BARRIERS

One of my more memorable lessons in leadership was really a lesson in communication. I had reported aboard my first ship and was assigned as the division officer of the Repair Division. My chief, a damage controlman chief (DCC), was a tough and unpleasant man. He was gruff, and I remember the first morning at quarters, as I was addressing the small division, he essentially ended my words for me, "That's great ensign; it is time to get to work." He was hard to communicate with and shared very little information with me. He ran a good show, but I realized I needed to get through to him if we were to truly succeed as a team. I racked my brain on how to break through to him.

One Saturday night in port, we had duty together. I went down to the machine shop with two cups of coffee (I didn't drink coffee back then) and just hung in the shop with him. We ended up talking about my family cranberry farm and my father being a career firefighter. That night started a softening of one of the toughest men I ever met. A week later, he asked me if I'd authorize him to come in late to work; I said yes without even asking why. It happened two more times, and in both instances I said yes. Of course, I was curious what he was up to, but I didn't ask. (What I learned later was that he had been building a car for several years and was finally ready to get it registered.) A few weeks went by, and to my great surprise, my chief invited me to his house on a Saturday. I was stunned, as were some of the other chiefs who had heard.

I brought two six packs of beer, was five minutes early, and was stunned, yet again, with what I found. Chief wanted me to be the first person to go for a ride with him in his new car. Both his sons played string instruments and showed off their huge encyclopedia collection. This man who I feared in many ways, a tough damage controlman who used to weld boxcars in New York on the midnight shift, was far more complex than I'd given him credit for. He was all the things I thought he was, but he was also well read, thoughtful, and passionate for learning.

The lessons I learned stick with me to this day: (1) Never, ever judge anyone. (2) Find common ground (there's always *something*). And, (3), in what became the biggest leadership lesson for me, through listening, observing, and communicating, you can always build a rewarding relationship.

—*RDML Ted LeClair, USN*

THE SLOWER YOU GO, THE SMALLER THE DENT

As a reserve lieutenant, I spent six weeks aboard the yard patrol boats in Annapolis participating in midshipmen summer cruises. A Merchant Marine captain led the program as reserve commander. He told me that "the slower you go, the smaller the dent." Now that I am captain of a nonprofit medical-aid vessel operating in the South Pacific, I remember that advice nearly every time I bring the ship alongside a pier.

But it also applies in other areas. Sometimes even when proceeding with deliberate caution, you still have to respond nearly instantly. For instance, you see the ship responding in an unanticipated direction, and you have to rapidly determine what force is at your disposal to correct the situation: a mooring line, the rudder, more power or less, a tug, and so forth. And then you have to use that force appropriately. Going too slow can also be dangerous in some ship-handling scenarios.

But proceeding with deliberate caution is nearly always appropriate. You get an email that makes you angry—do you blast right back with an emotionally charged attack leading to a relational shipwreck with a coworker, subordinate, or even boss? Or do you leave it in your inbox overnight and reply the next day with greater objectivity and rationality? Going slowly in your communications and relationships at every level reduces the dents you make on other people as you learn how to handle your own responsibilities.

Take time to get to know and understand your people and to listen to them. It will make your maneuvering as a leader much more effective. As a third mate on a cargo ship, my captain had spent many years as a chief mate. He told me that the hardest part of his job was to let the chief mate do the job he was supposed to do. Now as a captain myself, I really understand that. Especially when you were good at a job you used to have and enjoyed it, it is tempting to jump in and try to do a job that is now assigned to someone else. That is a pretty fast way of undermining and demotivating your people. If you can do the job yourself, why do you need them? And if you don't need them, why are they there? People want to be in a place where they feel they are making a significant contribution. Besides that, if you spend too much time trying to do the jobs of other people, you will wear yourself out, eventually getting to the point where you don't even do your job well. You have to be willing to trust your people.

—*CAPT Jeremy Schierer,*
master of a nonprofit medical-aid ship

DELEGATE 'TIL IT HURTS

You must master the art and science of delegation. Delegation is good for a number of reasons:

- It develops your subordinates.
- It frees you to do higher-order, more important work.
- It increases the total throughput of you and your team.
- It builds in you the ability to lead larger teams and organizations.

But for many, delegation is not natural. Too many young officers are reluctant to delegate because they are afraid their subordinates won't do it right. Some underdelegate and try to run the world themselves. Some overdelegate and try (or appear) to do nothing. Some delegate the wrong things and spend their remaining time on other, wrong things.

The most common problem, however, is underdelegation, either from fear, insecurity, a sense of control, or, sometimes, a sense of ego. Thus, I tell young officers that they must "delegate 'til it hurts." In general, push tasks down to your subordinates as much as humanly possible to free up your time to do the things they can't do. How much is enough? You're delegating about right when it starts to hurt. It'll hurt in three ways:

1. You'll feel uncomfortable. You'll wonder if your people can do the task as well as you can.

2. There will be mistakes. But if you aren't delegating enough so that your crew occasionally makes mistakes, then you aren't delegating enough! The key is to ensure the mistakes are small and caught in time. Mistakes are the result of people learning and doing new things.

3. You'll be envious. There will be times when the task is a fun or exciting one, something you'd like to do. But if it's more appropriate for one of your people to do it, suck it up and delegate! For instance, if a dignitary is visiting the ship and giving your organization an award, you'll want to give the tour and receive the recognition. But, better yet, assign the role to one of your junior people—let her bask in the glory. She will enjoy it and will feel proud for having been given the responsibility.

If you aren't hurting—at least a little—then you aren't delegating enough. And if you're not delegating enough, you can never grow fully into the leader you want to be.

—*RADM Robert Wray, USN (Ret.)*

CHAPTER 5

TAKING CARE OF PEOPLE

⚓

The true leader serves. Serves people. Serves their best interests, and in so doing will not always be popular, may not always impress. But because true leaders are motivated by loving concern rather than a desire for personal glory, they are willing to pay the price.

—*Eugene B. Habecker*

Being a leader is more than just wanting to lead. Leaders have empathy for others and a keen ability to find the best in people . . . not the worst . . . by truly caring for others.

—*Henry Gruland*

You've got to give loyalty down, if you want loyalty up.

—*Donald T. Regan*

Trust men, and they will be true to you.

—*Ralph Waldo Emerson*

Leaders must always put their people before themselves. If you do that, your business will take care of itself.

—*Sam Walton*

Leadership is not about being in charge. Leadership is about taking care of those in your charge.

—*Simon Sinek*

*T*aking care of your people is the foundation of leadership. Without their passion, nothing will get done well. Passion in one's work isn't something that can be forced, demanded, or ordered. It is a flame that must be carefully lit from another flame. Leaders demonstrating their passion provide an opportunity for that flame to be passed along to others. Passion does not always have to start from the leader either. Many already have passion. The leader's role is to find subordinates' passion, their motivation, and what they value in order to "speak their language" when encouraging performance. As the stories in this chapter demonstrate, the more you as a leader can take care of the people in your charge, the more those individuals will find passion in their work. Investing in your subordinates' futures, communicating with them frequently, and taking the opportunity to understand their background and experience are all paths that allow you to take care of your people. The first step is always making an effort to understand who they are.

WE HAVE TO TAKE CARE OF OUR PRISONER

I was in a great mood. My fellow SEALs and I were lodged safely behind a concrete wall about to call in our extraction helicopters. It seemed likely we would all return safely from our first combat mission.

Our mission was to capture individuals designated as "high-value targets" (HVTs). Although our HVTs weren't at our target that night (it was what we call a "dry hole"), we had executed our complex mission well. All my first-time-in-combat fears—will I survive, will I be a coward, will I mess up and look bad in front of my troops (a SEAL's worst fear)—were all going away as I crouched triumphantly behind that wall.

Tim, our team leader, observed some legs in camouflage trousers sticking out of a guard shack. "Roger, go check that out."

Crap. My great mood evaporated. I grabbed my team chief, Tom, and two first class petty officers, Jeff and Frank. We jumped over the wall into an open field in the center of a city block.

I assumed we'd find a corpse. We had taken small-arms fire on insertion, and our helo crew returned fire ferociously. Instead, we found an enemy soldier, unharmed and aiming a pistol vaguely in our direction. The dude was terrified and clearly harmless. Jeff easily relieved him of his pistol and, with Frank's help, escorted him out of the shack and laid him down in the grass. They both took up security positions while I held security on our prisoner. Tom shouldered his rifle and knelt down to search and secure him.

As Tom was finishing up, I took a moment to look around. We were surrounded by apartment buildings and hundreds of unlit windows. Just as I was thinking, "Huh, there could be a sniper in any one of those windows," we saw three or four muzzle flashes and then bam, bam, bam. Without much thinking, I took a couple of steps backward to put a brick column between me and the shooter. Frank and Jeff took similar measures.

Tom's response was different. It was also remarkable and inspiring. Tom instinctively laid his body over the prisoner's to protect him from errant rounds.

"Tom," I hollered, "we need to get out of here."

"Roger," he responded with a surprising, almost annoying, composure, "we need to take care of our prisoner."

"Okay, Tom, let's take care of him on the other side of that wall."

A good case study contains a lesson. Placing a prisoner's safety above your own may not be the lesson here. Tom's actions, I think, were above and beyond. But Tom's extraordinary empathy and humanity point us in the right direction. An enemy combatant, whether he voluntarily surrenders or is forcibly taken prisoner, is no longer an enemy combatant. He is out of the fight; "hors de combat" is the technical term. The prisoner assumes a new moral status and the capturer assumes a new moral obligation. Our prisoner had recovered his right not to be harmed. We had acquired the moral obligation to transfer him safely and with dignity from the battlefield to his "benign quarantine."

Here's the lesson: anyone who mistreats a prisoner, a person rendered essentially powerless, is a coward and a bully. Anyone who kills a prisoner is a murderer. Full stop.

GEN Douglas MacArthur penned these words in 1945: "The soldier, be he friend or foe, is charged with the protection of the weak and unarmed. It is the very essence and reason for his being." Tom, my team chief, courageously lived them that day.

—*CAPT Roger G. Herbert Jr., USN (Ret.)*

KNOWING YOUR PEOPLE

My skipper just informed me that he was making me the squadron's next quality assurance officer. As a first-tour naval aviator, this would be my first chance to serve as a division officer. I was chomping at the bit and immediately set out to put into practice the lessons I learned observing the maintenance officer on my first helicopter detachment. I got familiar with my "Sailor's Division Officer" folders and scheduled initial interviews. Up first was my leading petty officer, AD1 Jones. Jonesy had eighteen-plus years in the Navy and clearly held the respect of the Sailors in the shop. My first pitch was, "What can I do to help you make Chief?" I brought up ways to study for the exam and considered if a midtour award might help. These efforts were met respectfully but with little enthusiasm. I was frustrated; what was I doing wrong?

After a couple more conversations, where I started to listen more than I talked, I learned that Jonesy was extremely fulfilled putting his technical expertise to use and mentoring the junior Sailors but didn't want to be a chief. He wanted to retire at twenty years and get a job that capitalized on his Navy skills. Once I understood this, my focus shifted to helping him prepare for retirement and find that next job—help he enthusiastically accepted. It turns out not everyone wants the same thing from the Navy or in life, so listen to your Sailors. Find out what they want, not what you think they want, and make their goals your priority. Six years later, I had the pleasure to visit Jonesy at a depot-level maintenance facility where he was keeping our fleet of helicopters flying as a government contractor.

—*CDR Mike Norton, USN, PhD*

DECISIVE ACTION

As a newly minted officer of the deck (OOD), I spent most of my time on bridge watch. After my bridge team had established a professional rapport, a cross-decked ensign was assigned to my bridge team. On one particular watch, the cross-decked officer casually turned to the conning officer and junior OOD (JOOD) and began making racially charged statements directed toward me loudly enough for others to hear him. Despite repeated warnings, he continued to share his opinions until his watch relief arrived. Our amicable working environment was abruptly ended when he broke the solitude of our dwindling watch with the racist statements.

By early evening, word of the incident had spread like wildfire throughout the wardroom. When our commanding officer (CO) caught word, he acted swiftly, ordering the bridge to drive aggressively toward land. At 2200 that night, my CO manned the boat deck and sent that officer ashore.

The next morning, he assembled the wardroom and had a frank conversation with us about his professional standards. He reminded us that we were a family and that disrespectful language was unacceptable in our home. I found myself, like many others in the room, in awe of the magnitude of his leadership. He had just given us a lesson that we would never forget: leaders must act quickly to identify and eradicate toxicity at the source. If ignored, these behaviors can threaten the basic principles of leadership and the essence of a team.

—*Anonymous Lieutenant*

FORTUNE FAVORS THE BOLD

As a young division officer, I was the main-propulsion assistant (MPA) and Boilers Division officer on a frigate. I had over twenty outstanding and extremely hardworking boiler technicians (BTs). One of our real superstars was a first class petty officer (BT1) who was one of our two automatic boiler controls experts ("ABC Techs"). Our BT1 was the greatest, and our new captain knew it.

As we prepared for our operational propulsion-plant exam (OPPE), a tough exam that would reflect greatly on our nonengineering-background captain, we maintained our plant and trained our watchstanders relentlessly. As we prepared to go to sea one final week to run engineering drills before the OPPE, our superstar BT1 approached me with a leave request. Like most ships, our policy was that you didn't ask for nonemergency leave when we were going to be at sea. But our superstar's young wife was due to deliver their first child that week we would be at sea, and he "really wanted, really needed" to be there.

The boilers were controlled automatically by a mechanically complex system of low-pressure "control air." We knew that an important drill during the OPPE would be "Loss of Control Air." The BT1 owned this system; his potential absence meant that if we had a real control-air casualty we could not fix ourselves at sea, we would miss our last chance to practice that critical drill before the OPPE.

Understandably, the chief engineer (CHENG), executive officer (XO), and captain thought the BT1 needed to be at sea doing his critical job and that his wife would be fine in San Diego, if she did deliver that week. The BT1 was devastated and protested that his backup, a younger Sailor (a BT2), was qualified to do the job. Being young myself and not fully appreciating the professional pressure my superiors were facing, I decided to go back up the chain of command and plead the case directly to the captain.

The captain, to his credit, said, "Alright, MPA, we'll leave BT1 behind, but you had better hope those ABC's work, or else!"

So we left BT1 behind. During the first set of drills at sea, we sustained an actual control-air casualty. Our frigate went dead in the water and began rolling heavily. The BT2, under pressure, dove in and fixed the problem! And it turned out that BT2 was a true ABC genius whose talent had never been known because BT1 was so good.

That Friday afternoon as we came alongside the pier, BT1 was waiting, smiling broadly and holding his new child in his arms. As the brow was opened, BT1 handed his tiny new baby to his wife and bounded back aboard like a man possessed. He spent every remaining minute before the exam grooming his ABCs to the point that he was polishing the control-air lines themselves! And BT2 was right alongside him, inspired by his recent "victory at sea." Together they delivered; the examining team said it was "the best ABC system they had ever seen."

It was only the first of many times in my career leading Sailors that, when I accepted risk to my success for their benefit, I was rewarded beyond what I could have imagined. Leadership lesson: if you take care of the Sailors, they will take care of the ship . . . and you!

—*VADM John Christenson, USN*

COULDA, SHOULDA, WOULDA . . . DIDN'T

Sometimes our best lessons in leadership are ones learned through mistakes. Such was the case for me aboard my first ship. I was a newly minted division officer serving on board my first ship, a destroyer, in the Pacific. I was the Gunnery Division officer in charge of about twenty-five Sailors. One afternoon while I was making rounds about the ship, I noticed shouts, screams, and laughter coming from the berthing compartment. Realizing that berthing compartments were where the Sailors lived and slept, officers generally did not go in there except for during normal daily inspection times. With that in mind, I knocked on the door, and the noise immediately stopped.

My eyes darted around the room, trying to assess the situation. I saw a bunch of big guys holding one other smaller guy back—was it a fight? They all looked at me as if they were in trouble, and my spider sense tingled, but I just didn't know what was going on. A few seconds later, I heard, "Hey, sir, nothing going on here, just having a little fun." I said something like "I hope not," but felt like this was not my place and this was just a bunch of guys having fun. I was very wrong.

A few hours later, as I was walking by sick bay (the onboard medical clinic), I noticed that one of my gunners mates was there with a corpsman (medic) tending to his arm—severely bruised, discolored, and grotesquely enlarged. As it turned out, he was a victim of hazing that involved members of his division punching him in the arm as hard as they could, one after another, to "celebrate" and "tack on" his new rank insignia on his sleeve. Apparently, he was the sailor being held back in the berthing. I was sick to my stomach.

Seeing my sailor suffer what could have been permanent injury, as well as the obvious pain, is still to this day one of my biggest regrets. While I had never heard of this type of hazing, in hindsight, I clearly missed an opportunity to intervene. I could have asked more questions or disbanded the group, and I didn't. And I vowed from that day forward never to be a bystander again.

I let my Sailor down. To this day, I think about him standing there—hoping his new division officer would say something. And I think about this whenever I am asked to give leadership lessons to young officers. You *will* be confronted by situations where your gut tells you something isn't right. Our best leaders are those who are ready for those circumstances and think how they would act *before* things happen—we call that forehandedness. You need to be ready to act quickly and resolutely, as the opportunity window to act closes as time passes. How will *you* respond?

—*VADM Ron Boxall, USN*

COMMAND ADVANCING A SAILOR

The Command Advancement Program (CAP), similar to today's Meritorious Advancement Program (MAP) process, allowed a ship's CO to promote, or advance, a Sailor, even if he or she hadn't achieved test scores high enough for regular advancement. This is the story of the most memorable command advancement I ever saw. A boatswain's mate second class had taken the test to be advanced to first class at least a dozen times and had passed the test, but he hadn't achieved high-enough scores to be advanced. He was a recognized leader in his division, department, and on the ship. He had qualified as OOD (underway) and was by all accounts performing well above his paygrade. The Command Advancement Board met and the decision was easy.

The question was: How to execute the advancement? The common way I have seen it done in the past is to wait until the results of the latest advancement exam were published and then command-advance the deserving Sailor that passed but didn't get advanced. But I wanted to do something better for this Sailor. So, on the day of the first class exam, all the second class were on the mess decks taking the exam. Shortly after it started, we mustered the crew on the fantail. We then sent for the BM2 to be pulled out of the exam because there was some catastrophe that only he could deal with on the fantail. Of course, the BM2 hopped right up; after all, the ship needed him! He popped out on the fantail and saw the crew but still didn't know what was happening.

The captain signaled the BM2 over and asked what he was doing. When he replied that he was taking the advancement exam, the CO asked, "Why are you doing that? You're already a BM1!" The crew burst into applause, and the BM1 got all choked up. It was a great day for all and a great way to take care of a great Sailor.

—*VADM Tom Rowden, USN*

THE SINKING SHIP

It was a cold winter night in the middle of the Mediterranean. About midnight, we received a distress call from a

Greek freighter en route to Libya; she was sinking. We sped to her location and found the crew already getting into life-boats. As their ship slumped lower in the water, we hauled them on board our Navy cruiser. We launched a boat to circle the sinking freighter. Her crew had seen flooding in the engine room—they couldn't find the cause, so they abandoned ship. We Navy engineers were chomping at the bit to go on board, to go below, to find the problem, and to resolve it. We felt we could save the ship, if the captain would only let us try.

But the captain wouldn't buy it. The Greek crew had already abandoned the ship. The shipping company would be compensated by insurance. The cargo was cement—not too precious to be replaced. He couldn't see risking his crew to save this freighter that nobody else seemed to care about. We young engineers thought he was being a conservative old man; we muttered under our breath that he should let us do our job. We pressed him; he still said no.

As the night went on, we stood by, and we continued to circle the vessel in our gig. Just around dawn, suddenly and without warning, the stricken freighter stood up on one end and plunged into the sea. It happened in a minute or less. If we had been inside, we never would have gotten out. After that, we young engineers were glad that our captain had been as conservative as he had.

I learned two lessons. First, sometimes being conservative is the right thing to do, even if others don't think so. Second, don't risk your people unless it's something worth risking them for!

—*RADM Robert Wray, USN (Ret.)*

BUILDING ESPRIT DE CORPS

While serving as strike officer aboard a guided-missile destroyer, we had just transited the Strait of Hormuz for the final time on our way home to San Diego when the USS *Cole* was bombed by terrorists off the coast of Yemen. After six extremely tense hours stopped dead in the water in the Gulf of Oman, we were told to turn around and retransit the strait, where we spent the next forty-five days back inside the gulf with a daily mission status of "To Be Determined." Our deployment was originally supposed to return to San Diego right before Thanksgiving, but as Thanksgiving neared, we still had no idea how long we'd be extended. As you can imagine, morale was deteriorating, and there was not much we could tell our friends and family about when we'd be heading home. Finally, after weeks of waiting, we were ordered home to San Diego, scheduled to arrive on December 23.

Since we were arriving so close to Christmas, I thought that we should do something special. In the wardroom one evening, I suggested to the captain that when we manned the rails at Sea and Anchor detail, we should have everyone wear Santa hats and play Christmas music over the ship's general announcing system (1MC). The rest of the wardroom, mostly male, groaned and said that it wasn't manly. The supply officer (suppo), of course, said that it would be impossible to get three hundred Santa hats, that it would be too expensive, and that he didn't have time to contract it out; he used every other excuse possible. However, after several days of pitching my idea, the captain finally told the suppo to "make it happen." The Santa hats were purchased and loaded on board during our fuel stop in Hawaii. I will never forget how fun and exciting it was to come around the bend under the Coronado Bay Bridge, perfectly clear blue sky with a warm Santa Ana breeze, everyone topside in Dress Blues and bright red Santa hats, blasting "Santa Claus Is Coming to Town" through the 1MC. The families loved it, the kids were so excited, and it was such a simple and easy gesture.

Moral: Sometimes it's necessary to push past the naysayers to help build esprit de corps. The little things really do matter and can do wonders for crew morale. To this day, I still remember how special it was the day "Boats" blew the whistle and shouted "Moored," and two Sailors in Santa hats shifted colors.

—*LCDR Nicole Maver-Shue, USN*

THE SAILOR AND HIS SON

Being tested in theory and being tested face-to-face are worlds apart. I found that out one day as I served as an ensign stationed aboard a guided-missile destroyer. We were steaming off the coast of the Falkland Islands during the United Kingdom's war with Argentina; the stakes were high, and the needs were great as our ship stood at the ready to move into combat, when and if necessary. I was in charge of the seventy Sailors in the Boiler Division, ranging in age from seventeen to fifty-three; I wanted the team to stay tight for this important operation.

One of my Sailors, a boiler technician petty officer third class, came to see me privately. He was upset; his five-year-old son had fallen off a swing set at a playground and had broken his left hip. The boy was rushed to a local hospital, where emergency surgery would be necessary to insert rods and pins into his bones. The petty officer went on to say that he was divorced and did not have custody of his son because he was in the Navy on sea duty. He said the incident was affecting his work and focus on the job at hand. I continued to listen to him as his voice wavered and as a look of helplessness encompassed him. It was clear that coming to me had been a difficult decision under the circumstances. As my Sailor concluded our private conversation, he then shared the underlying, lump-in-his-throat reason that he had come to speak with me—his son had a rare disease that caused brittle bones.

What's an ensign to do? I began an internal balancing test: Supporting my Sailor might make my department head boss unhappy because of the importance of the mission. Not supporting my Sailor meant keeping my division intact but potentially risking mistakes and errors in judgment due to distraction. I found myself reaching deep down inside to do the right thing. I made the decision to send my Sailor home to be with his son. I felt that his son would not remember the mission we were on in years to come but would remember that his father was by his bedside when he recovered from his surgery. I was committed to this Sailor, as I was to all my Sailors, to do what was right in a time of need, even when the mission might be affected and even when I, as an ensign, was being tested.

As we know, tests provide feedback. When my Sailor returned, he made it a point to let me know that he held a debt of gratitude. He gave me his total commitment and would do whatever was needed to support me. He rejoined the other Sailors in the division with a renewed focus, sharing that the ensign was someone who cared. Sometimes it's tough to balance the mission and the people. I believe the answer rests, as it did here with my Sailor on that day, in taking care of our people in order to take care of our missions.

—*RADM Kelvin N. Dixon, USN*

SAFETY FIRST

Military Sealift Command is a large organization with more than a hundred ships. A couple of years ago, we had a shipboard accident with a man-lift that killed two people. They weren't following proper procedures; after the accident, we spent considerable time re-educating our ten thousand people around the world on safety issues, particularly with man-lifts.

During that period, I spent a lot of time on our ships talking to our mariners. As I always do, I left them my email address in case they had any concerns they didn't want to talk about in the large group. A few days later, I got an email from an experienced mariner who had seen a man-lift on a nearby frigate operating in the same unsafe manner that had caused our accident years before. "I have a son the age of those Sailors on that lift," he wrote. "It would be sad to see anything happen to them, like it did to our guys."

He was afraid to bring up the safety issue to the frigate's crew because he thought an outsider from another ship commenting on their safety practices would be unwelcome. I told our mariner that it was everybody's responsibility to bring up safety issues and that I was positive the frigate's skipper would be happy to get any feedback he could to make his crew more safe. I called the commodore, who called the frigate's captain and relayed the issue about the man-lift. Sure enough, they were glad that our mariner had seen the issue and had reported it. (Even if he used an unusual route to report it!)

Moral: Some things, like safety, are just too important to worry about protocol and hurting people's feelings. You've heard the phrase, "Everybody is a safety observer." It's true. If anybody sees anybody doing something unsafe, particularly with something that can kill people, they should report it. And damn the consequences.

—*RADM Robert Wray, USN (Ret.)*

MAN OVERBOARD!

I was CO of an aircraft carrier. We had just completed a lengthy major overhaul and were scheduled for a five-day at-sea period for postavailability sea trials. The flight deck was not yet certified for flight operations, and no helicopter-support detachment for search and rescue would be available for our sea trials. This meant that I would be restricted to a boat recovery in the event of a man-overboard situation. The weather forecast was generally favorable, but with periods of unusually heavy seas and high winds. These conditions would make small-boat operations impossible. I decided that we would proceed to sea under these conditions despite the potential risk.

After two days of routine sea-trial events, I signed my night orders and noted that the strengthening wind and increasing seas would make night boat operations hazardous if not impossible. I spoke to my command team and then addressed the crew on the 1MC, cautioning them that I had limited options for man-overboard recovery, and I directed the closure of weather decks to all nonessential personnel.

At roughly 0200, my worst nightmare was realized with the call: "Man overboard, starboard side, away the ready lifeboat!" I was quickly joined on the bridge by my XO as we maneuvered to create a lee for possible boat deployment. My first lieutenant called from the starboard sponson aft to report the rigid-hull inflatable boat (RHIB) and crew were ready to be lowered into the water. Given the weather conditions, I was reluctant to put the boat and its eight-Sailor crew at risk in a nasty sea. As I was deliberating, the XO looked me right in the eye and said, "Captain, we have a report of two lights going over the starboard side into the water. The lookout was unable to determine if there were bodies attached to those lights." Then came the most chilling report of all. "Captain, we have two men missing from muster. Both were seen on the flight deck, starboard side, moments before the lights were seen going overboard."

I now had two good reasons to believe I had two crew-members in the water. Their survival time, given ambient temperatures and high winds, was less than an hour, even if they had good flotation. There was no helicopter-rescue option. If there were men in the water, only my boat and rescue crew could recover them. Every moment that I delayed a decision to deploy the rescue boat lowered the survivability chances of my two missing crew. On the other hand, dare I risk eight Sailors in an attempt to rescue two?

How could I *not* take that risk, knowing two were in peril on the sea?

I asked for professional advice from the XO and first lieutenant. First replied, "We can do this Captain! Let us go get our guys!" Of course, the first was looking at relatively calm seas created by the lee of a 90,000-ton aircraft carrier. From the bridge, the XO and I could see the true wind strength and increasingly choppy seas outside of the ship's lee. I made my decision in seconds: "First Lieutenant, lower the boat."

No sooner had I received the report, "Boat is away, Captain," when the XO rushed to me to report, "Captain, all crew members now sighted and accounted for!" If I really didn't have a potential tragedy before, I sure had one now, with eight Sailors alone in a small boat on a dark night in angry seas. And I had put them there.

Outside the protection of the carrier's lee, my small boat and eight Sailors were being pounded to pieces. I ordered them to return to the ship for immediate recovery, an order they eagerly obeyed. It took seven unsuccessful approaches before we could get the boat secured to the hoist and raised, but the boat was eventually recovered safely.

I greeted the crew as they came off the boat. They were soaked to the skin, freezing cold, and absolutely terrified. I called them all together because I wanted them to understand why I had risked their lives needlessly. All were respectful, but my search-and-rescue (SAR) swimmer dropped his gear on the deck, said, "I quit," and never stood SAR swimmer duty again.

Despite making logical, defendable decisions each step of the way, in the end I was backed into a corner in which my decision placed eight priceless lives at unacceptable risk. I had made what I thought was the right decision at the time with the information I had. I had every good reason to believe that I had two men in the water when I launched the boat. If that had in fact been true and I had *not* made an attempt to save them, I would have been forever unable to forgive myself for my inaction and would be worthless as a captain to this ship and crew. In the same situation again, with the same information, I would lower the boat again.

What's the leadership lesson? First, you have to understand that what can go wrong, will go wrong. I should have lobbied more strongly for onboard SAR helicopter support. Second, Mother Nature is a merciless lady, never to be underestimated or trifled with. Third, if you do not decide, facts will decide for you. I had no option to gather more information. If there were men in the water, delay meant possible death. Fourth, and perhaps most importantly, only the senior officer on the scene can make these command decisions, and any officer must be morally prepared to face a choice as I had to. Once the decision is made, it's yours and yours alone. You will be held totally accountable, forever, for choosing wisely—or not. I was lucky, and I didn't lose anyone. Such is the responsibility and total accountability of leadership at sea.

—*RDML Ronald H. Henderson Jr., USN*

THE ENSIGN IN THE SNOW

My first lesson in leadership and motivating people came just after I graduated from the Naval Academy. While waiting for my start date at Nuclear Power School, I was assigned temporary duty to Portsmouth Naval Shipyard as an assistant ship superintendent to a submarine in overhaul. It was winter in New Hampshire on the waterfront; it was cold! I was an understudy to a very salty and well-respected limited duty officer (LDO) who was very savvy about getting things done. One night on the graveyard shift, a system had a part failure. It was serious—if not fixed quickly, it would delay the test program and thereby possibly keep the submarine in overhaul longer than planned. I called the Supply Department, and they said they would bring someone in from home to draw the part; as long as they had an officer sign for it, the paperwork could be completed the next day.

Before I left to go to the Supply Building across the yard, a worker came in and said they had found a way to fix the system without the new part. I sank down in my chair and let out a big sigh of relief, since now I wouldn't have to walk all the way across the snowy shipyard. However, the LDO had other ideas. He said, "Get up right now, hustle across the yard and pick up the part. Thank the supply folks like they were saving your life, and bring back the part. We can turn it back in tomorrow." I protested, not liking in the least the idea of trudging across the yard in the cold and snow. The LDO looked me in the eye and asked, "What will they do the next time you call, Ensign?" I learned an important lesson—people will go above and beyond to make things happen, but you better make sure they know their efforts are appreciated if you want it to happen more than once.

—*RDML William Timme, USN*

DANGER TO LIFE AND HEALTH

I was the leading chief petty officer (LCPO) of Repair Division on board the USS *Blue Ridge* when we discovered a leak in the engine room along the aft bulkhead adjacent to a collection, holding, and transfer (CHT) tank. Upon further investigation, we discovered that the leak led directly into the main header for the tank and through the bimetallic bulkhead sleeve. This type of repair was well beyond the capability of ship's force and needed depot-level attention. In order to properly isolate the leak and conduct the repair, the entire aft CHT system needed to be tagged out and secured, which affected the health and comfort of all aft berthings. This is not what the chain of command wanted to hear at the time, especially our CHENG.

In two weeks, the shipyard came in and cleaned the tank but left residual sewage in it. There were small traces of hydrogen sulfide but nothing outside of the limits of exposure levels with a self-contained breathing apparatus (SCBA) on. From there, the CHENG ordered us to commence the cleanup of the leftover sewage and start repairs. With the proper safety gear donned, we commenced the cleanup; but instantly, hydrogen-sulfide levels began to rise. Within minutes of the work, the level rose above the immediate danger to life or health (IDLH) limits. This prompted an instant evacuation of the tank and surrounding spaces.

The damage control assistant (DCA) and I briefed the CHENG of the situation and the measures that needed to take place, but his response was, "Just get it done, they will be fine with just SCBAs."

This is where we put our foot down. His orders would have put Sailors at risk of death, first by having one source of breathing air, and second by allowing an IDLH space to be open to surrounding spaces without proper ventilation. We told him that we wanted CO approval before we moved forward with the proper procedures for the cleanup and removal of the toxic gas and would not move forward the way he directed.

It took this act of standing up to do things the right way regardless of consequence that made him realize he was making a poor decision. We regrouped with the help of the shipyard and were able to remove the sewage, remove the hydrogen sulfide, and get a depot-level repair completed. The CHENG later apologized for his actions and was thankful that the DCA and I were willing to put Sailors' safety and doing the right thing over his clouded judgment of just wanting to get the job done. We weren't just concerned for the well-being of our Sailors; we were also helping our leader make sound decisions. As a leader you must learn that is it your duty to support up and down the chain of command.

—HTCS (SW/IW) William Sisk, USN

CHAPTER 6

FORCEFUL BACKUP

⚓

No one will make a great leader who wants to do it all himself, or to get all the credit for doing it.
—*Andrew Carnegie*

The best executive is one who has sense enough to pick good people to do what he wants done, and self-restraint enough to keep from meddling with them while they do it.
—*Theodore Roosevelt*

A good leader encourages followers to tell him what he needs to know, not what he wants to hear.
—*John C. Maxwell*

*F*orceful backup is the deliberate, anticipatory, and timely action taken to prevent improper and potentially catastrophic events from occurring. No individual, which includes the boss, can see or understand everything happening in dynamic and rapidly evolving events. High-functioning teams rely on everyone, no matter the person's seniority, to speak up when a member sees something that might cause damage to the ship and/or injury to the crew. In cases where the observer believes that the perceived threat will cause great harm, the concept of forceful backup requires immediate and effective action to prevent such a disaster from happening. It is the responsibility of the leader to create a climate in which forceful backup can occur.

This often requires a deliberate discussion on the topic with the team, ensuring that everyone knows the expectations for forceful backup. *Humility* is a key ingredient in the leader for this concept. Leaders must understand that no matter how many years of sea time or how many evolutions they've conducted, they are human, make mistakes, and simply just can't see everything as it happens. The following sea stories, told by senior officers whose bacons were saved by this concept, demonstrate how even the most respected leaders can be humbled and reminded how important forceful backup is. The maritime environment is unforgiving and requires constant vigilance at all levels to accomplish the mission safely. Fostering a climate of forceful backup is essential in saltwater leadership.

NEVER ASSUME THE CONSEQUENCES ARE KNOWN

A Sailor should never assume that someone senior has thought about the consequences of their actions because this might not be the case. A Sailor, no matter what rank, could save a shipmate's life or avoid serious harm by simply asking the question, "Should we be doing this?" This mindset of safety and risk mitigation paid off in full when I was the commanding officer (CO) of an Aegis guided missile cruiser. One night, we had to put the port rigid-hull inflatable boat (RHIB) in the water.

The first lieutenant, an ensign who had been on board a few months, was the conning officer. I was on the port bridge wing when he was setting the ship up to create the lee for the boat launch. Once he thought he had found the lee, he said we were ready. I looked down, noticing the lee was a little too rough. I said, "Hey first lieutenant, let's come over about another twenty-five more degrees to get the seas a little smoother."

He said, "Aye, aye, sir!" and ordered left five degrees rudder. The ship was at five knots. I said, "First, I'd like to get this done before next week."

"Aye, sir, increase your rudder to left full!" he said.

Just then, somebody interrupted me with unrelated admin work. I ignored them, checked the lee, then said, "First, this is good." He replied, "Aye, aye, sir."

The entire ship knew I did not do admin work on the bridge; I only did bridge work on the bridge. That person interrupted me again, and I asked him to leave the bridge wing.

The last thing I heard the conning officer say was "aye, aye, sir." In my mind, that meant that the conning officer had steadied up on course. I turned to the officer of the deck (OOD) and said, "Put the RHIB in the water." The RHIB was already at the rail and loaded. The OOD ordered the RHIB to be put in the water. As the RHIB was being lowered into the water, a quartermaster third class poked me in the back as she said, "Captain, we still have a left full rudder on!"

How many ships are there in the Navy where a quartermaster third class can poke the captain of an Aegis cruiser in the back to tell him he's making a mistake?

What's going to happen if that RHIB hits the water with a left full rudder? It's going to flip over, and six people would have gone into the water. I immediately said, "This is the captain; I have the conn. Shift your rudder," and with that, as well as having great boatswain's mates, the boat landed in the water safely and drove away.

The quartermaster third class saved lives that day. The reason why she saved lives was because she did not assume that someone senior had thought about the consequences of an action. It was everyone's duty to speak up. She didn't hesitate to poke me in the back. After RHIB operations were complete, my knees stopped shaking, my heart rate came down from about 180 to 95 beats per minute, and my adrenaline abated. I walked down to my cabin, grabbed a Navy Achievement Medal, walked up to the port bridge wing, and put it on her.

The lesson of this story is that she did not assume someone senior to her—even I as the captain—had thought about the consequences of an action. She recognized the danger and took action to provide forceful backup.

—VADM Rich Brown

DELIVERING BAD NEWS

As a lieutenant, I was the assistant navigator on an aircraft carrier getting ready to go into the shipyard for about three months. I was tasked with overseeing the entire crew's work package; I was responsible for all the work the crew would do. The captain had a reputation for a quick temper but was universally regarded as an outstanding commander and officer.

Before the shipyard period, the captain called a meeting in his stateroom for the other officers who would play a major role in this maintenance period. Each of the other officers, all very senior to me, gave their reports stating that all the work would get done and that it would be the best shipyard period ever. When he got to me, I told him I was very concerned that each department, particularly engineering, had bitten off more than they could chew. I presented a list of over one thousand items that the Repair Division said they would do in the coming three months. I told the captain that I had doubts as to whether this could be done and that I'd work with the repair officer to prioritize what needed to be completed.

He glared at me, and I thought I was in trouble. He then faced the other, more senior officers and said that this was exactly what he wanted to hear. While not doubting any of the other reports, he stated that if we had bad news, then he wanted to hear it! He would rather know ahead of time than be surprised in the end. He demanded total honesty from us all and never once shot the messenger. This made the whole shipyard experience a pleasant one for me professionally, and for the ship in general.

Lessons I learned: First, give your bosses bad news, even if you think they won't like it, because they need it to do their job. And second, if you want your folks to give you the bad news you need to know to do your job, don't shoot the messenger! If you do, they won't give you bad news, and that's not good for you or your ship.

—*CDR Ted Kramer, USN*

LOOKING AWFUL SPORTY!

I was a brand new captain, CO of a fleet oiler and a career fighter pilot in deep-draft command as part of my nuclear-power track. I was confident in my ability to drive the ship, and even though she is 50,000 tons, I had not quite learned to be a little more gentle in her maneuvering. I guess you could say I am an aggressive ship driver.

On this particular—very black—night with no moon and calm seas, we were in the western Pacific and steaming in company with the USS *Carl Vinson,* commanded by CAPT Rick Wren, where I served as executive officer just two months prior.

I wanted to gain plane-guard experience for my junior officers, so several weeks before this night, I asked Rick if he would have the strike-group staff task my oiler as plane guard during day and night flight ops. We received tasking to assume plane-guard position as we returned to the group following a brief stop in port. My plan as captain was to shoot *Vinson*'s stern and maneuver sharply to starboard to roll in nicely one thousand yards astern, matching her speed. In this case, I warned the OOD to not fall into long trail behind *Vinson* and add power to catch up; use "lead" to drive right to the desired plane-guard position. So, I had her point the oiler's bow ahead of *Vinson*'s.

I was seated in the captain's chair on the bridge, monitoring the rendezvous. That chair was offset from centerline by a few feet to port, so my vantage point was left of the bow, skewing my assessment of the bow's position such that it appeared to me to be pointed farther aft of *Vinson*'s beam than it actually was. As we passed five miles closing, the OOD sidled up next to my chair, started to show me a maneuvering board, and said, "Sir, we need to come to port; our intercept is too hot. We are pointed forward of her beam."

I responded, "No, we do not need to come to port, maintain your heading. This is called 'lead' with our bow pointed ahead of *Vinson*'s beam." Remember, I do not want to look bad to my former CO on the *Vinson* by falling in trail too far. The OOD, momentarily returning to the Navy table and reviewing the maneuvering-board solution, came back to my right side and said, "Captain, I recommend coming to port fifteen degrees. We are on a collision course."

About that time the CO of the *Vinson* keyed our common frequency on the radio and said, "Lookin' awful sporty!" Of course, being the aggressive captain that I was, with recent experience as his partner on *Vinson*, I replied, "Yessir!"— not catching the meaning of his transmission. My assessment was that we were maneuvering aggressively but would nicely roll into position behind *Vinson* without touching the power. I did not recognize that the oiler was on a clear "constant bearing, decreasing range" (CBDR) course, partly due to my desire not to look bad and partly because I was seated in an offset position that masked the actual geometry as I looked out the window.

We were then less than two miles from *Vinson*, CBDR.

The OOD comes back and in a very strong voice says, "Captain, I am ordering left 30 degrees rudder to avoid collision with *Vinson*!" I jumped out of my chair, stood on the centerline, ready to countermand her order and, with a jump of my heart, realized we were in fact CBDR with almost no time to maneuver!

I ordered hard left rudder, and as the ship heeled hard to starboard, we passed down *Vinson*'s starboard side at fewer than one thousand yards. As we passed her midships I ordered, "shift your rudder to right full," and swung the ship's stern away to cross *Vinson*'s wake at five hundred yards astern.

For the rest of the night's operations, which included *Vinson* repositioning between flight ops events, I relied on the OOD's maneuvering skill to keep us in position. I never once made a recommendation to her. I have told that story many times, citing the OOD's professionalism and ability to speak truth to power as *the key factors* that saved us from a devastating collision.

The intended lesson for all junior leaders is to be confident in your skills and your procedures, assuming a strident position of authority when standing watch. The intended lesson for captains is beyond what I have described here. The lesson is to set limits for your watchstanders that are inside of your own limits. As captain, you can *never* exceed your limit, because there is only *one person* who can get the situation back under control, and that is *you,* with no backup.

—*RADM Mike Manazir, USN (Ret.)*

STICK TO YOUR CONVICTIONS

While conducting operations during Operation Desert Storm, the USS *Tripoli* struck a mine that opened a twenty-five-by-twenty-three-foot hole below the waterline on her starboard side. As a lieutenant commander in command of a minesweeper, my crew and that of my sister minesweeper were tasked with conducting an immediate search around the vicinity of USS *Tripoli* to determine a path to lead her out of the minefield she now found herself within. After approximately fifteen hours of searching, we determined a way out of the minefield and proposed to the mine-warfare commander, a Navy captain, the track that we intended to lead *Tripoli* down.

The mine-warfare commander told us that his staff did not agree with the track and directed us toward a different path. Having just searched the waters and knowing for certain that the new track would cause further damage and possibly sink *Tripoli,* I got on the radio and painted a picture of what we saw during our search along that track. I told the commander that I saw with my own eyes on sonar a moored mine case and chain, much like the mine that *Tripoli* had struck. The mine-warfare commander replied that he would trust me and go with our track.

Over a four-hour period, the *Tripoli* was led out of the minefield, following one thousand yards astern of my minesweeper. *Tripoli*'s maximum speed was four knots to prevent the forward-machinery-space bulkhead, which "panted" at higher speeds, from failing. The minimum speed was three knots as *Tripoli* lost steerageway below that threshold. After *Tripoli* was safely clear of the minefield, the CO of USS *Leader* and myself received a personal message from the mine-warfare commander stating that his staff had misplotted some mines and that *Tripoli* would have hit another one had we not done our jobs so well.

The lesson learned is that even if you are a junior officer, stick to your convictions, especially if lives are at risk, and be convincing without being disrespectful.

—*CAPT David Jackson, USN (Ret.)*

THE SKIPPER IS ALWAYS RIGHT (NOT REALLY!)

I remember the night as if it were yesterday. I was a brand-new lieutenant (jg) with a brand new skipper. We were pulling into port, and I was the Sea and Anchor conning officer and had a rather impish OOD. The night was calm—no wind, perfect visibility, and more importantly, nobody on the pier. The skipper was just coming off a three-year tour at the Pentagon and, in his own words, was "rusty, but ready to proceed with no witnesses." His simply stating this should be an indicator of what a great leader he was and is. As we began our approach, the skipper took the conn and clearly stated that if anything "comes up" that I should take the conn back immediately. (Another sign of a great leader.) Our approach was uneventful, and the entire Sea and Anchor detail was at ease despite having the skipper driving.

As we made our final lineup on the pier, the radio blared that we were to shift to a new berth; this would now force us to dock between the rocky quay wall and another ship preparing to get underway in the early morning. Not too tricky, but enough changes in a short time span to force some critical calculations to be completed quickly. The first approach was very short. The second attempt was a little slower, but didn't get us close enough. Unfortunately, at this point the tension was rising just because the skipper was trying so hard and just not landing it. He stayed positive, cracked a couple jokes, and backed us out again. By now, I had great situational awareness and had had so many Sea and Anchor details on board that I could have done it with my eyes shut. A thought flashed through my mind: "Do I offer a couple of tips about the ship's handling, or just keep quiet?"

Then the most unexpected thing happened. The skipper asked me what he was doing wrong! The bridge erupted in smiles, all tension was gone, and I felt more at ease to offer suggestions. I told him it takes a while after a long break and that it was a tricky approach. I recommended he leave the speed up a little longer just so we had some steerage way as we cut it. Not surprisingly, he heeded my advice, and on the next approach, I had to recommend that he slow down a little bit. He did, and his confidence increased as we just missed the perfect landing. The skipper had one more shot in him, and he knew this would be it. Unfortunately, the "bubble" was lost during the final backing out, and the skipper got a little rattled. As we made the final approach, he wanted to make certain he had enough speed to land it. As we completed the backing, he adjusted speed up just a little too much, and the jagged rocks were now approaching too fast. I looked at the skipper, and with just critical seconds remaining, he simply looked at me, nodded, and stepped back. I immediately announced I had the conn, ordered "emergency back full" and "right full rudder." We avoided the rocks, docked, and took a deep breath. Then I mockingly called up engineering to cancel the divers for the hull inspection. There was silence until the skipper chuckled, smacked me on the back, and the crew finally exhaled.

The safe docking of the ship is not the moral of the story. It is the skipper creating an atmosphere of trial and demonstrating to the crew that it was acceptable for them to do the same in their workspace, with similar safeguards.

It taught me and everyone else on the bridge that night to fully understand all situations and speak up when things are turning perilous.

—*RADM Scott Jerabek, USN*

WATCH-TEAM BACKUP

The transit from the city of Portland, Oregon, to the open sea via the Columbia River is one of the longest and most challenging Special Sea and Anchor details a bridge team will face. With a distance of over one hundred nautical miles, this section of the Columbia flows at about three knots, which means a vessel steaming downriver must make turns for about eight to ten knots just to maintain bare steerageway. Narrow at many points, full of meeting situations, and several sharp turns, this evolution is a complex ship-handling event.

On this transit, I learned the crucial importance of having a forceful watch-team backup. What is meant by this is that, no matter the rank or position an individual has on the team, each member needs to be able to speak up in a strong, clear, unemotional, and direct way to tell the entire team that something is wrong, there is a potentially hazardous situation developing, or, if need be, step into someone else's role. This all must be carried out in an instant so that appropriate action may be taken by the whole team in order to avoid an incident.

While transiting down the Columbia River in an *Austin*-class LPD, I was the OOD and had on my team a young but qualified conning officer, a master helmsman, a lee helmsman, a helm safety officer, a boatswain's mate of the watch, and several lookouts and phone talkers. In addition, the captain was in his chair on the starboard side of the bridge, and the river pilot and navigator were on the port side. About halfway through the transit, both the conn and I noted that the vessel was a bit right of track and was edging toward the right bank of the river. At my direction, the conn gave the order "left five degrees rudder," and the helmsman answered "left five degrees rudder, aye," and applied *right* five degrees rudder.

Being a good conn, when he gave the order, the conning officer was watching the rudder angle indicator above a bridge window, saw the error, and immediately gave the command "left ten degrees rudder," which the helmsman responded with "left ten degrees rudder, aye," and put the helm over to another five degrees *right!* At this point, the bow was now pointed toward the right bank of the river. The captain, who had been watching this error chain unfold, ordered "shift your rudder," which the helmsman did and swung our rudders back over to left ten degrees. I then announced, "Captain has the conn," and the captain ordered "emergency all back full" on both engines. As we were a steam ship, in addition to being pushed along by the river, this action alone would not be enough to keep us from grounding. The captain then ordered "let go the ready anchor," which the phone talker relayed to the forecastle. Looking through the bridge window, I saw no movement by the anchor detail. Realizing that the order had not been received, I grabbed the 1MC mic and passed "let go the ready anchor." This alerted the anchor detail, who immediately tripped the pelican hook and let go the port anchor. By this time, the astern bell had been answered, and the props had started to bite. The anchor hit bottom and the brake was set, at which point we felt the anchor skip along the river's bottom. After a few seconds of smoke from the anchor brake and the shuddering of the stern as the props bit, the ship came to a stop in the river *without* grounding.

Once stopped, the captain, the conn, and myself all exhaled audibly, and the helmsman and helm safety officer were relieved and sent below. The captain passed the conn back to the conning officer to resume our transit. From the captain having the situational awareness of the developing issue between the conn and the helm to my observation of the breakdown in communications between the bridge and the forecastle, the error chain was severed, a grounding was avoided, and several careers were saved. The lesson is that when mistakes happen—and they will happen—it is a team effort in backing up each other in order to avoid catastrophe.

—*CDR Steven M. Wendelin, USN*

CHAPTER 7

CULTURE

⚓

> Expect people to be better than they are; it helps
> them to become better. But don't be disappointed
> when they are not; it helps them to keep trying.
> —*Mary Browne*

> It's amazing how much you can accomplish if
> you do not care who gets the credit.
> —*Harry Truman*

> Nobody cares how much you know, until they
> know how much you care.
> —*Theodore Roosevelt*

*C*ulture is the central element of the informal organization of each group, unit, team, and command. The formal organization consists of the chain of command, how subgroups are connected, and who works for who, all of which can be easily depicted on an organizational diagram. As most know, however, there is much more to teams and organizations than this. The informal component consists of the culture and climate of the organization and imparts significant influence on the effectiveness and efficiency of the team. Culture is the system of shared backgrounds, norms, values, or beliefs that drive the members' behaviors. Climate is how members repeatedly react within this culture. They are interrelated and can be driven top-down by the leader as well as bottom-up by dominant members of the group. Although culture and climate are difficult to visually depict on a diagram, there are four major artifacts that are readily apparent: myths and stories of the organization, symbols, rituals, and jargon. These artifacts are not the culture itself but evidence of the culture that resides within the organization.

The culture consists of shared values that transcend many situations. It is very difficult to change quickly, requiring consistent communication by leaders and the members of the organization. A leader provides intentional and unintentional communication that establishes a culture with everything they do or do not do: personnel policies and promotions, feedback and coaching, how they act both normally and under pressure, and what is talked about or goes unspoken. In the absence of a culture directed by the leader, one will develop nevertheless from the direction of dominant members within the group. Every organization has a culture. How it occurs and if it aligns with the stated mission and task of the organization can vary radically. The stories below address how a unit culture was established in some small way. They depict one event to represent many events that occurred over time to set the organization's culture. As these sea stories make clear, it's everyone's responsibility to form their organization's culture.

THE AFTERMATH OF THE PARTY

As a lieutenant, I was the commanding officer (CO) of a Coast Guard Island-class 110-foot Patrol Boat (WPB).

During the end of an in-port period, our sixteen-member crew (minus me and the executive officer [XO]) held an off-base party that spiraled out of control. Before the evening was done, I had crewmembers who were assaulted, several others who committed underage drinking or contributed by allowing underage drinking, and one crewmember who was arrested for driving while intoxicated. Our unit was preparing for a thirty-day patrol to Haiti and was due to depart our homeport in only three days. My XO hastily completed an investigation so we could dispose of any charges before the deployment.

The day we were to leave on patrol, I held Captain's Mast on four crewmembers at 1000. The rest of the crew served either as mast representatives or as witnesses to the various offenses. The four nonjudicial punishment proceedings concluded around 1300. We were scheduled to depart that evening from Naval Station Roosevelt Roads, Puerto Rico, at 2000 in order to make our arrival time in Guantanamo Bay, Cuba. The events of the past seventy-two hours took a mental strain on our entire crew, myself included. I felt a nighttime outbound transit was riskier than normal with a crew whose collective thoughts may not have been focused on safe navigation. I elected to contact my O-6 commander in San Juan and requested a twelve-hour delay in sailing until 0800 the following morning. My request was approved.

I learned three lessons from this. First, while it would have been simpler due to the breadth of the disciplinary infractions and our upcoming patrol to merely lecture the crew on their personal responsibilities, I learned that each member had to be held accountable for their actions, even if it was uncomfortable for me to provide that accountability. Second, I also learned that as CO, if my head wasn't completely focused on the upcoming task at hand (night transit), I shouldn't put my ship or crew needlessly at risk. We were all able to get a good night of sleep, clear our collective cobwebs, and depart port the next morning safely in daylight. By slightly adjusting our transit speed, we were still able to arrive for relief on time. And third, I learned that one should clearly articulate to their supervisor if they are not 100 percent capable of carrying out their duties for any reason.

I am proud to report that in the more than one year I had remaining on my tour, I had no further problems with alcohol by the crew and no additional Captain's Masts.

—*RDML Christopher Tomney, USCG*

REMEMBER YOU'RE PART OF SOMETHING BIGGER

When I checked into my first duty station, I was so ready to finally be "in the fleet." The whole time working with our officer-selection officers throughout officer-candidate school, during the Basic School and Military Occupational Specialty (MOS) School, we were assured over and over that the environment we were currently in was "not the fleet." It was supposed to help us appreciate—or at least more willingly accept—many of the more controlling and supervisory aspects inherent in a training environment. But it also generated anticipation for that time when we would be the independent, self-policing, autonomous leaders that all this schooling and training was designed to make out of us. Indeed, one of the first things I noticed within the first week or two, before I was assigned to lead my own section, was how relaxed peers who had arrived six months to a year before me were. As junior officers, we were assigned to shared offices, where most of us kept our uniforms to change into after arriving and departing in civilian attire. Several of my peers had a consistent routine of strolling in around 0730, socializing until about 0800 before changing and executing the plan of the day, and then taking a two-hour lunch to conduct physical training, to shower, and to eat.

Considering that to be an inefficient use of time, and never having seen anyone take accountability or seen any of the officers check in with someone by a specific time to confirm their presence, I simply began working out and showering in the morning, arriving in the office by 0800 to begin work when everyone else apparently did, and then took only a short lunch, resulting in much greater productivity.

Unfortunately, I didn't communicate my plan. One day the boss asked where I was, and my (not so helpful) officemate responded that not only did he not know but also that I had been showing up late every day. Fortunately for me, when my boss later called me in to discuss the matter, as a good leader, he led the conversation by making sure that everything with me was all right—if there was some external event or situation he should be concerned about that was causing me to be late. That in itself was a great demonstration of leadership, that he led with concern for my well-being instead of assuming wrongdoing based on the initial comments from my officemate.

In addition, once I explained my routine, he completely understood and passed on some advice that I became much more attuned to when I became a section head and again as a member of a commander's staff: the military is both a very large institution and very reliant on accountability and readiness, so there will be many processes that benefit the organization at the expense of individual efficiency. For example, in the context of my workout routine, even though it was more efficient for me, granting individuals discretion to set their start times this way would have impeded the ability of the unit CO to account for all his personnel each morning. To be sure, I still found ways to achieve greater efficiency with my time, but it was a valuable reminder that I am part of something bigger than myself, even as an officer and a holder of special trust and confidence within "the fleet."

—*Capt Evan Field, USMC*

TRUST YOUR PEOPLE, THAT'S WHY YOU HAVE THEM

Prior to commissioning in the Navy, I was an enlisted aircraft mechanic in the Marine Corps. During my last deployment, I was the maintenance control chief for the AV-8B Harrier detachment on board an amphibious assault ship. My primary duties included ensuring each aircraft was airworthy and capable of providing fixed-wing combat capabilities for the 15th Marine Expeditionary Unit (MEU).

Nearly halfway through the deployment, my officer in charge (OIC) tasked me with putting together a team to survey the conditions of Al-Jaber Air Base in Kuwait for a potential four-week training evolution with the Kuwait Air Force. The base had never housed Harriers before, and the boss was concerned that the facilities would not support our daily operations. I dispatched a team of senior enlisted maintainers from each of the three major work centers to conduct an assessment. There was easily over forty years of experience among the three maintainers.

After returning from the survey, the team informed me that not only was the base ill-equipped to support any major maintenance evolutions but also the runway itself could be a potential source of engine damage due to the poorly kept flight line. The team briefed the OIC on what they discovered while I explained the pitfalls of having to conduct major maintenance evolutions on the base. After listening to each of his most experienced maintainers and maintenance control chief, the OIC decided to disregard our recommendation and proceed with the training evolution over our objections.

Within one week of operating on the base, we discovered that all six of our aircraft had suffered irreparable engine damage from loose rocks breaking off the runway. With the proper equipment, support, and facilities, one Harrier engine change could be expected to take about a week; that time was doubled in Kuwait. Our four-week training evolution ended up being a loss of close air support for the MEU for over ten weeks. Ultimately, our OIC was relieved and sent home while the Maintenance Department was left to figure out a way to remove and replace a total of seven AV-8B engines before the ship's planned departure from the area.

I could have easily sided with my boss, knowing how much he wanted to conduct this "first time" training, but I opted to trust the experienced maintainers who were there to ensure the safe operation of the aircraft. Had the boss done the same, he likely would not have been relieved for the upward of $7 million worth of costs associated with removing and replacing the damaged engines.

—*LT Anthony Couch, USN*

WE DON'T DO PAPERWORK

As the Maintenance Department's quality assurance officer, I relished flying daily, troubleshooting interesting problems with the helicopters. I was excited to come to work each day! One Friday, the skipper told me that I was moving to the Administration Office (Admin) as the squadron's junior department head. On Monday, I met the chief yeoman, who had just arrived. We would get to know our team together. My brief from the Admin team was simple—"we don't go home until our in-boxes are empty." The mantra was "keep the paperwork moving." That motto was hard to get excited about!

The XO's and CO's offices adjoined our office. Admin's highest priority was quickly completing tasks the XO and CO needed: messages formatted, letters typed, phone calls handled, and other duties. Their boss expected the squadron's executive business to be prompt.

But in my year in the Maintenance Department, I had heard a recurring complaint: the Sailor standing at the service counter in Admin was a low priority. During that first week with the team, I observed a young Sailor with his wife, standing at the counter, trying unsuccessfully to make progress on his check in. Each time someone started to help the couple, "urgent business" would pull that person away. The service counter was closed for lunch, which was the only time for the maintainers to climb off aircraft to take care of their Admin concerns. It looked like our priorities were skewed. The new chief shared my concerns and made a keen observation: that the yeomen, personnel staff, disbursing clerks, corpsman, and legalmen "wanted to do better for the Sailors. We need to define and clear the path."

After the chief met with our team, they forged a new standard: success would be measured by how well we served the "youngest Sailor in the Squadron." The Sailors' needs would be our primary focus. We discussed our goal with the XO and CO, who enthusiastically supported the effort. A new mantra was prominently displayed: "We don't do paperwork . . . we care for Sailors." Our petty officers developed a new procedure for documents generated by Sailors. A team member took ownership of each document. That person tracked it through all required stages. The team member then took it to the Personnel Support Detachment on base, over to the Disbursing Office, to the Medical Clinic, or wherever it needed to go. One day I asked for "Airman Jones's paperwork" and was informed (with good humor), "Sir, we don't do paperwork!" Then the responsible petty officer stepped up with an up-to-date report on Jones's promotion and pay raise. We ate lunch early or late so that from 1130 to 1300, we would be at full strength to work the service counter.

A week or so later, our disbursing clerk suggested that if he worked in the Disbursing Office two days each week, he could audit our two hundred pay records before deployment, likely finding errors that could be fixed in our Sailor's favor. He found thousands of dollars that way! Our corpsman jumped on that idea. He would work out of the hospital on Tuesdays and eliminate the backlog of medical appointments for our Sailors and their dependents. Again, a huge win! Now empowered to act on their own ideas, the Admin team members executed several great programs on their own initiative. Their enthusiasm (and mine!) grew each month. And I learned some lessons:

1. Invest considerable time with the chief.
2. Ensure your team members understand their mission and know who they are: "We don't do paperwork. We care for Sailors!"
3. Don't under estimate how *great* your Sailors want to be. Empower them to be their best selves.
4. Embrace every job you are assigned. The Admin job turned out to be an incredible leadership (and life) lesson.

—CAPT Jim Pendley, USN (Ret.)

BEING HONEST WITH THE BOSS

I was a SEAL task unit commander at SEAL Team One, and one of my two platoons was attending jungle-warfare training in the swamps just outside of New Orleans in preparation for our upcoming deployment to the Philippines. The platoon had been conducting reconnaissance in a nasty, alligator-infested swamp on the edge of the base for about a week, reporting on "enemy" activity near the Tactical Operations Center, where I was situated. Every other day, since I knew from their reporting exactly where they would be, I would sneak out with my task unit chief and observe the platoon from a distance for a few hours.

I noticed that platoon members were never seen cleaning weapons, which was alarming given how dirty the environment was.

Once the platoon ended training and we regrouped for the debrief with the training staff, my task unit chief and I planned to bring up the dirty weapons as a major issue with the SEALs. As the platoon came into the classroom and stacked their weapons in the rear, I quickly did a cursory inspection, which confirmed that the weapons had been untouched and would most likely malfunction quickly if fired. Just as the debrief was about to begin, the CO of the SEAL team and the command master chief walked in unannounced to observe the debrief and our follow-on training.

Although I didn't want to highlight such a negative point for the platoon in front of the CO, it was bad enough that something had to be said during the debrief. I went ahead as we had planned and discussed in length what we observed and, without highlighting individuals, pointed out the rifle muzzles that were plugged with mud in the back of the classroom. We also highlighted the number of things the platoon did well during training. After the debrief, two members cornered me about how they felt betrayed that I would call out any negative points in front of the CO.

Months later, during our deployment to the Philippines, the skipper provided a very large amount of autonomy to our task unit to conduct operations, often delegating his own authority down to my level. When I was seeking approval on a particularly delicate operation, the CO brought up the dirty weapons during jungle-warfare training as a major source of his trust in our task unit.

Bringing up the negative as well as the positive points of our training in front of the CO earned us a great deal of his trust, which was very helpful during our deployment. I'm convinced that had we only brought up positive points in that debrief and in later conversations, the CO would not have had the same level of confidence in our unit to police ourselves, which would have resulted in considerably more oversight while overseas. It was months later during our deployment that I, along with the two SEALs who had felt betrayed, understood the benefit of bringing up our own deficiencies in front of the CO.

—*CDR Andrew Ledford, USN*

IS IT HOT OUT HERE?

December 4, 2014, was a relatively cool day by Djiboutian standards. The temperature hovered in the mideighties after the sun set. It was also the day that I took command of Camp Lemonnier Djibouti (CLDJ), the only permanent U.S. military installation on the continent of Africa.

During my ten-day turnover, I had become intimately familiar with the complex system that provided the life-sustaining, mission-essential water for the camp's more than 4,500 personnel. The daily weather report for CLDJ was fairly straightforward: it was either hot, really hot, or damn hot. Needless to say, water was everything. When I assumed command, I inherited one of the finest Civil Engineer Corps officers in the Navy as my public works officer (PWO). He had been in-country for over six months by the time I arrived. He knew the base infrastructure inside-and-out.

The three most important buildings at CLDJ were several wells responsible for bringing water up from a modest aquifer several hundred feet below the surface. Each well consists of a pump that drops down a long shaft, submerges into the aquifer, and forces enough brackish water to the surface and into our reverse-osmosis water purification unit (ROWPU) to sustain the camp. Since the day I arrived, we had been having some issues with one of the pumps in the wells. It needed to be replaced. So what better thing to do on my first night as CO than watch my talented public works team remove and replace the pump?

By the time I arrived at the scene, the repair operation was in full swing. My outstanding PWO was standing next me, explaining the process and patiently answering every one of my stupid questions. Initially, I was fascinated. Over the next hour or two, it grew boring, but I decided to stay as a show of solidarity with the team. It was at that point that I realized my trusted PWO had completely sweated though his Type IIIs. He looked like he had stood in the shower. My only thought at the time was, "Is it hot out here?"

Just after 0200, the malfunctioning pump had been removed from the narrow shaft that had been its home for the past year or so. By sunrise, the well was back in service. While all of the wells were important, this one was the shallowest and by far the most productive. As a result, the water it brought to the surface was the easiest to purify. It was also used to bring a majority of CLDJ's lifeblood out of the aquifer. I did not understand the consequences of mission failure as I stood by that night watching the operation. If that well had become inoperable or even worse—if the pump had become fouled and rendered the well permanently out of commission—the camp would have immediately gone into water restrictions until repairs were made or a new well had been drilled. That could have taken months. Non-mission-essential personnel would have been evacuated immediately. Operations critical to our national security and regional stability would have been negatively affected. Thankfully, my PWO understood this. He trusted his team, and I inherently trusted him. Every one of us will reach a point in our careers at which we will no longer be able to serve as the subject-matter expert over an aspect of our command's mission or operations. A good leader must recognize this sooner than later; do everything in his power to ensure that his teams have the tools, training, and authorities necessary to accomplish the mission; and then possess the strength and confidence to place his unequivocal trust in them to accomplish the mission.

—*RDML Matt O'Keefe, USN*

THE VALUE OF SECOND CHANCES

In 1995 my first ship, a guided missile destroyer, was in a dry dock in Norfolk, Virginia, making postdeployment repairs. I had joined the ship two months earlier in the Arabian Gulf. Assigned as the antisubmarine warfare (ASW) Officer, I was consumed that week with getting my team trained and certified at the ASW trainers. While at the trainer, I received an urgent phone call that a hurricane was heading for a direct hit on Norfolk, and the dry dock had already started flooding. I rushed back to the ship. My most important task was to pressurize our two rubber sonar domes. My chief sonar technician supervised the work. I looked on for hours, not knowing much about how the system worked. We screwed it up badly. A few days later, we learned we had done extensive damage to the sonar transducers and dome structure. A major dry docking was required to effect repairs.

A formal Judge Advocate General investigation ensued and resulted in my receiving a nonpunitive letter of caution. I had failed in my duties in many ways. I did not pay attention to the deteriorating weather conditions and the effect on my ship. I failed to use operational risk management and develop a contingency plan prior to going into dry dock. I failed to properly supervise a critical evolution for which I responsible, regardless of my lack of knowledge or training. I did not know how my equipment worked. The results of the investigation hit me hard—I was absolutely certain my career was over.

Years later I realized just how wise and patient my captain had been. He gave me a nonpunitive letter of caution, worked on my shortfalls, and eventually developed me into a competent surface warrior. This captain gave me a second chance, and it changed my life. Your Sailors are human beings and will also make mistakes; be generous with those second chances, and do your best to develop their full potential!

—*RADM Brian L. LaRoche, USN*

RAISING THE STANDARDS

I joined an Aegis cruiser as the XO while it was on deployment; it didn't take long for me to figure out that there was room for improvement. The passageways were dirty and dingy, brass wasn't shined, fire stations weren't properly stowed, papers were taped up to bulkheads, and so forth. And as I started doing daily messing and berthing inspections, I found the berthing compartments and heads to be dirty, racks not made, and gear adrift. So, taking a page from the "start hard" playbook, I got the department heads and command master chief together and told them the ship was unsatisfactory and they were going to help me get it squared away. I started formal passageway inspections, with each space presented by the Sailor who owned it and with the divisional chief petty officer (CPO) and division officer present.

These were very tough inspections to a very high standard: perfect cleanliness, brass shined, everything perfectly stowed, all damage-control gear in place and properly stowed, watertight doors perfectly maintained, and so on. I would do the ship in sections to keep the inspection duration reasonable while allowing time for a detailed assessment. When a day's inspection was over, I would get on the ship's general announcing system (1MC) and announce the "Best Passageway" winner, "Best Shined Brass" winner, and other such awards, giving credit to the division and department and often the individual Sailor who owned the space. The results were instantaneous and dramatic. Within a month, the ship shined and department heads, division officers, chiefs, and petty officers were trying to outdo each other in the "Best Space" competitions.

I did the same thing for berthing compartments, obtaining the same results. Once I had the ship up to that standard, it stayed that way for my entire twenty-month tour. The lesson is: start out strong, set high standards, insist that people meet your standards, and find positive ways to motivate your people.

—*RADM Kevin Quinn, USN*

BREAKING THE GENDER BARRIER AT DIVE SCHOOL

In November 1979, I reported to the Navy School of Diving and Salvage in Washington, D.C. Diving and salvage was considered one of the more challenging pursuits for a newly commissioned ensign; I was one of the first three women to attend diving school. The Mark V diving rig weighed 198 pounds, and the mixed-gas rig weighed a whopping 300 pounds. And, of course, a school that starts in November and graduates in May in Washington, D.C., translates into a long winter of diving and tending in the cold, icy Anacostia River. On the first day of school, Chief Youngblood met me with a roar, barking out, "I bet you don't last a week in this school and I'll make sure you don't." I accepted that bet. For a week, he took great pleasure in riding me during long morning physical-training sessions and seemingly endless runs to the pool. By the end of the week, I had had enough and snapped back. But as we all know, students don't have the right to yell at an instructor. I paid dearly with a massive amount of penalty pushups and eight-count body builders, but I had made it to the end of the week and did not quit. The chief paid off his bet with a smile and said, "I knew you would make it."

The chief probably singled me out because the diving school was unaccustomed to women students at a time when the Navy was still "adjusting" to new opportunities

that had been opened to women. His attitude infuriated me
to success. However, the real leadership lesson occurred in
the twenty-two weeks that followed. He invested his time
and energies in teaching and mentoring me to ensure I
could meet the requirements of the school. He invested in
me and recognized the capability that could be cultivated.
At times it meant coming in on the weekends to do extra
work, but he invested himself in the effort. To this impres-
sionable ensign, he showed that leadership is about selfless
devotion to duty and a willingness to invest in the success
of others. Whether he agreed with women entering his
world of "Navy Diver" was unimportant; he encouraged
excellence and commitment because it was the right thing
to do, regardless of my gender.

—*RDML Martha Herb, USN*

THE DIRTY LAUNDRY

My first fleet job was as a lieutenant (jg) pilot. I was new
to the squadron and assigned to the Maintenance Department. I was flying and was in the office when I wasn't in the
air. I was a Branch Head—I had only one subgroup of the
one hundred maintainers in the squadron.

I had a master chief as my branch CPO. A less naïve
individual would have wondered why a master chief was a
branch CPO and not the leading CPO of the entire department. Because of flight schedules, twelve-hour missions,
and detachments for several days at a time, I was seldom in
the office. I relied heavily on the chief to tell me how things
were going and what needed to be done. Of course, the
answer was always that everything was under control. Over

time, I got to know many of the thirty or so troops in our branch; one flew on my crew. None, of course, was going to tell the mostly absent lieutenant (jg) about the dirty laundry. Only after we didn't do very well on an annual maintenance inspection did I find out that, if I wasn't aboard, the chief was gone to the club by 1000 and drunk not long after that. He was a pretty functional alcoholic, so when I did see him, he seemed like a solid, low-key fellow who knew his job. I didn't have enough savvy to ask all the right questions.

So what is the leadership lesson? First, for the rookie, don't try to reinvent the wheel. Ask for guidance from someone senior enough to provide it. Asking for education is not a sign of weakness. People love to be asked for their opinion. Seek a lot of them.

Second, pay attention and do the job you're assigned to do. I wanted to fly; I viewed my maintenance job as a lesser priority. If I had paid more attention to that job, which was also important, I would have recognized the master chief's problems earlier.

And third, if there's dirty laundry, expose it! The senior officers in the squadron knew about the master chief and his drinking problem. They should have warned me, the new guy. Better yet, they should have been dealing with it before I showed up. Not letting the rookie know did a disservice to the enlisted sailors in the branch.

—*RADM Casey Coane, USN*

NOT HAVING THE ANSWERS

As a member of shipboard fighter squadrons for many years, I saw many COs come and go. All of them had an

Officers Call on their first day in the job, but I can't say I remember what any of them said, except for one. This CO stood up in front of the ready room and said, "I know I'm in charge, but don't think I have all the answers." He struck a chord with me that I remember to this day, some fifteen years later. In fact, I have used those same words during each one of my four command tours.

With that one short sentence, that skipper set the tone for his highly successful tour in two ways. First, he created a command climate where new ideas and discussion were encouraged. He essentially said, "You people will know things I don't know, and I want those ideas." Second, he made all of us in the ready room feel that we could make an input and be part of the solution. What a great way to build a *team!* We all know the Navy is a military organization and the boss has 51 percent of the vote, but when people in a command get to make an input and feel that it is given due consideration, they will feel valued and more likely to support wholeheartedly the boss's final decision.

Most of us have worked, at some point in our careers, in an environment where our boss says, "If I want your opinion I'll ask you. Your job is to be seen but not heard." How did that make us feel? Did that stifle our desire to propose new ideas? Did we feel part of the team? One simple sentence, followed up by action, can create a positive atmosphere that encourages collaboration and team building and ultimately leads to mission success.

The moral of this story is when you get to your ships, tell them: "I know I'm in charge, but I don't think I have all the answers." Your people will be glad you did.

—*RADM John Sadler, USN*

LEADERSHIP BY UNINTENTIONAL EXAMPLE

I was a second lieutenant and the newest rifle-platoon commander of my Marine infantry company. My company was in Okinawa for a six-month deployment and spent each Friday morning on a "hump," a fast march, with our combat load. Each Marine would carry their weapon, body armor and helmet, and at least fifty pounds in their pack for the evolution. My platoon sergeant would randomly check our packs before each hump to keep the Marines honest on the weight. We started the deployment with three miles on the first Friday and worked our way up to twenty-five miles over the course of several months. Each hump was at a three-miles-per-fifty-minutes pace, with a ten-minute break per hour.

As the newest second lieutenant of the company, I often felt the need to prove myself to the other rifle-platoon commanders in the company, most of whom were first lieutenants. During one of these initial humps, I noticed that one of the other first lieutenants would check on his Marines during our ten-minute break first before he put down his pack for his own break. Not to be outdone, I began doing the same and would keep my pack on just a little bit longer than him to "prove myself." Although our platoons were often separated by a small distance, he quickly noticed what I was doing and began keeping his pack on for longer periods as well. By the next hump, neither one of us would drop our packs for any of the breaks as we walked around our platoons, chatting it up with our Marines, who were sitting along the side of the road. It became a friendly competition between us to see if either would drop their pack during any of the breaks. As the humps each week became longer and longer, fifteen miles, then eighteen, then twenty-one, this became quite painful for six to seven hours, as we would both forego sitting down or dropping our packs. We both walked the length of our platoons to ensure the other platoon commander could see we were still up and "comfortable" while our platoons sat exhausted, wondering why we were so chatty and unaffected by the hump.

It took me several weeks to notice, but my platoon (and his) noticed this as well, and the squad leaders soon began walking the line before taking their rest. They felt that if the platoon commander could give up his break to check on the platoon, then they should be doing the same for their squad. I never told them to do any of this, but the example of walking along the platoon before I took my own break, even though it was done in a competitive spirit with another junior officer, made a lasting impression. It was quickly picked up in other evolutions as well, such as setting defensive perimeters and digging fighting positions in which my fire-team leaders and squad leaders would finish digging out their positions and, before taking a break, would go and help others get their positions done.

Although it was leadership by accidental example, the lesson of checking on my Marines before I looked to my own needs was an early and valuable lesson in my military career. Each time I have practiced it in follow-on assignments, I've noticed that others around me replicated it as well.

—*CDR Andrew Ledford, USN*

CHAPTER 8

PROFESSIONAL COMPETENCE

⚓

[Officers,] be strict in your discipline; that is, to require nothing unreasonable of your officers and men, but see that whatever is required be punctually complied with.

—*GEN GEORGE WASHINGTON*

Leadership is a potent combination of strategy and character. But if you must be without one, be without the strategy.

—*GEN H. NORMAN SCHWARZKOPF*

High expectations are the key to everything.

—*SAM WALTON*

Success seems to be connected with action. Successful people keep moving. They make mistakes, but they don't quit.

—*CONRAD HILTON*

There are no secrets to success. It is the result of preparation, hard work, and learning from failure.

—*GEN COLIN POWELL*

You get what you inspect, not what you expect!

—*ANONYMOUS SEAGOING OFFICER*

It is imperative for . . . an officer to know his sailors. Get to know them—know their strengths, their weaknesses, their skills, their wisdom.

—*ADM ARLEIGH BURKE*

> I am a great believer in luck, and I find the harder
> I work the more I have of it.
>
> —*Thomas Jefferson*

Regardless of service, seniority, community, commissioning source, or rating, a leader will be evaluated by his or her Sailors on a daily basis. The degree to which he or she is able to establish and communicate *professional competence* in dealing with team members will contribute significantly to a leader's success. For the purpose of this chapter, we differentiate between *experience,* by which we mean a measure of tenure and duration, and *competency,* by which we refer to an ability to perform the tasks and skills associated with one's profession at a level of quality and speed generally found acceptable by one's seniors. Without question, the determinants of competency evolve over the course of a career—mastery of the skills associated with commanding a destroyer are, perhaps not surprisingly, very different than those associated with being a first-tour division officer. Regardless of where you are on your career journey, over the course of a career, you will realize the perception of a leader's professional competency ultimately becomes an enabler for high-performing organizations to excel.

The following collection of sea stories, offered by leaders of all ranks, specialties, and services, demonstrate in real-world anecdotes what professional competency looks like, why it's important, and why the continuing pursuit of credible, professional competency becomes an enabler for high-performing teams. In the development of teams, leaders who lack professional competency will struggle to garner the confidence of their members, while those who hone their craft throughout the course of their career to continually improve will unlock the great potential of their units, crews, departments, divisions, and selves.

TRAIN YOUR RELIEF

When I was in command of a nuclear attack submarine, we conducted a surfaced transit into Mina Salman, Bahrain. My crew and I had transited these waters before, and we were confident in our ability to safely pilot to the pier. But on this day, we found ourselves in the middle of a heavy shamal (sand storm), which significantly reduced visibility and made our transit much more challenging.

On the bridge with me during this transit was a qualified officer of the day (OOD) who, although very competent, lacked self-confidence. He knew the rules of the road well but often second-guessed his decisions in challenging situations. I was happy we chose him to pilot this time so I could help develop his skills and overcome his lack of confidence. This particular approach is a long, winding track between buoys—effectively a two-lane highway for large tankers. It is a very forgiving transit because there is good water outside the buoys. If we ever got ourselves in trouble inside the buoys, we could always go outside them to avoid danger.

Because of the shamal, the OOD made our small surfaced submarine more visible by running both radars, transmitting on the automatic identification system (AIS), and rigging radar reflectors. As long as we could be "seen," other vessels were more likely to follow the rules. This was a great decision by the OOD to minimize the risk of collision, but his plan also included transiting outside the buoys to maximize our distance to the large outbound vessels. Although his plan was safe, it wasn't one that would boost his self-confidence, so I disagreed and ordered him to stay inside the buoys.

As we approached the "highway," a very large outbound tanker appeared on our radar. This enormous vessel's bow broke through the shamal at about seven hundred yards, and we visually confirmed her position, navigation lights, and so forth. No surprises, but the OOD was *very* anxious. He recommended a maneuver to starboard to give the tanker more room, but I refused. I wanted him to stay the course to gain experience and confidence in operating close to large ships.

"What visual indications should we expect for a normal port-to-port passage?" I asked.

"Sir, we should continue to see the mast head light and red running light, but the green running light should extinguish," he correctly replied.

"Excellent!" I replied. "What if the green running light doesn't extinguish?" I asked.

"It is an indication that the vessel is turning to port in front of us."

"Right again! See, you've got a handle on this situation."

Over the next sixty seconds, the OOD and I watched for the green light to extinguish, but it never did. The OOD frantically yelled, "She's turning toward us!" He was right! The tanker had failed to notice our position and blindly turned left—a clear violation of the rules of the road. The OOD put over a hard right rudder, sped up, and hailed the ship on the bridge-to-bridge radio. When the tanker noticed our position, she remained clear, and we passed nervously at about two hundred yards. The OOD had saved the ship!

Key takeaway: Experience at sea is the key to becoming a more competent and confident mariner. In order to grow, officers must work their way out of uncomfortable situations and recognize that, regardless of rank, a leader should continue to learn. Such experiences are not only valuable for them but also for the officers and Sailors they will some-day lead as their captain.

—*CAPT David Roberts, USN*

SPOT CHECKS

Preventive maintenance is one of the fundamental things we do in the Navy to ensure combat readiness. Our Sail-ors spend a lot of time and energy checking and double-checking the equipment we rely on. This program is very regimented and consists of very detailed procedures and a long-range schedule dictating when even the smallest maintenance check will be completed.

I have learned three valuable lessons over the years managing this critical program and doing spot checks. First, *do spot checks!* There are specific requirements for officers to observe Sailors performing maintenance, but these go way beyond just ensuring the checks are done and accounted for properly. Spot checks can give you a good idea of command climate. If Sailors are careless with admin and cavalier with execution, it may indicate a disengaged Chief's Mess or a prevalent "get it done at any cost" attitude.

Second, do more spot checks than prescribed. Preventative maintenance will consume the majority of a Sailor's time, depending on the rating, and as a leader, you should know where your Sailors' time goes. Is it wasted with unnecessary steps? Do they have the right tools? Do they have the parts and supplies they need? Take the time to make sure your Sailors aren't wasting theirs.

Third, spot checks are one-on-one time with your Sailors. Get to know them, ask them about their family, hobbies, advancement, training programs they want, and such things. Spend this scheduled time between you and the Sailors wisely.

Finally, do not be afraid to fail a spot check. Regardless of the reason, your Sailors will want to know you have standards that must be maintained. If you take this much time with them checking whether a light bulb works on a console, just imagine how much time and care you will take on their evaluations and awards!

—*CAPT Adam Fleming, USN*

NOT A GOOD PLAN

It was mid-December, and our carrier had been at sea for a month. We were excited to get home. Arriving in Norfolk, Virginia, we discovered that one helicopter needed a main-gearbox change. A chief and six maintainers, my copilot, and I stayed in Norfolk for a few days as the squadron flew home to Jacksonville, Florida. The job should require four days.

The main-gearbox replacement was a complex job. Connected to the gearbox were both engines, the main rotor, the tail-rotor driveshaft, three hydraulic pumps, two generators, two lubrication pumps, and the three primary flight-control servos. By Thursday morning, it looked like we would finish that evening, fly the functional check flight Friday morning, and fly the six-hour flight to Jacksonville Friday afternoon.

With a long Friday ahead of me, I decided to hit the rack by 2100. As I checked on things late Thursday, the crew was still working. Early Friday morning, an unsettled feeling began to creep over me. I had promised to be home for the weekend. The maintenance team had held up their end!

I knew that with the complex maintenance just completed, a six-hour flight had some risks. A single hydraulic, fuel, or oil line vibrating loose would require a precautionary landing. I realized I made a terrible mistake. I climbed out of the helicopter and explained to the chief that I had made a bad plan and an irresponsible promise. I would not fly with a new main gearbox six hours at night with passengers. The maintenance team was noticeably disappointed.

We would launch early Saturday. But before we slept, I would do one more thorough preflight. As I climbed up on the helicopter, something caught my eye. At the bottom of a primary flight-control servo, a cotter pin was missing. I put my index finger on the nut and spun it 3/4 of a turn. It fell off into my hand. I climbed off the helicopter shaking.

I handed the chief the nut. Though there is redundancy in the hydraulic systems, there is no redundancy in the flight-control linkage. If the linkage is compromised, as this was, the helicopter would be uncontrollable. Fortunately, the nut had stayed on the bolt long enough for us to complete the check flight. It is unlikely that it would have remained in place for the long flight home. We flew home safely on Saturday.

Lessons learned, and things I was not proud to tell the skipper:

First, "get-home-itis" had driven my bad plan. A daylight flight home should have been nonnegotiable.

Second, the same disease had caused the maintenance crew to work through the night.

Things that saved our bacon:

First, I paid attention to my intuition. Did I notice subconsciously that the crew looked unusually tired and inattentive? Did I notice that the work did not look up to our standards? Somehow I knew something was not right.

Second, I was willing to climb out of the helicopter as the crew was enthusiastically loading for the flight home and say, "Chief, I got this wrong." There will be times when you realize that you have made a bad decision or plan. Own it, and fix it. It will be humbling, but it will be important.

—*CAPT Jim Pendley, USN*

FIRST DEPLOYMENTS AND SECOND CHANCES

My first deployment began with our ship heading to the Red Sea to execute maritime interception operations. Our mission was to ensure that no illegal goods were heading to or from Iraq. When certain conditions were met, our ship would insert a boarding team on other vessels to ensure no illicit goods, weapons, or bad actors were headed to the wrong place. The ship's captain was an exacting commanding officer (CO) who was far more concerned about executing the mission than being loved. The close-quarters ship handling required in these operations felt like a varsity-level event to this young OOD. Not every boarding went perfectly, and the captain could be withering when I failed to measure up.

As the deployment progressed, I was tapped early to qualify as tactical action officer (TAO). The most senior watch position on the ship, the TAO oversees the tactical employment of the ship, guides the bridge team, and exercises weapons-release authority in the CO's absence. Since my ship was the senior ship in the three-ship task force, our TAO was also responsible for overseeing the entire operation in the Red Sea. In all, it was a fantastic experience for a young surface warrior.

It was also pretty heady stuff for someone still shy of his twenty-fifth birthday when the captain introduced me to our admiral as the "youngest TAO in the Navy who is running our operations in the Red Sea." I received a little ribbing from my pals for that, but this seemed like a small price to pay for such an incredible opportunity. Things seemed like they could not be going any better.

All this changed on a pitch-black morning watch in December. In what seemed like a matter of seconds (really a couple minutes), a merchant ship that had been drifting to save fuel near our ship's position sped up and improbably executed a 135-degree turn, crossing our ship's bow as it headed to a new position that had been arranged without our knowledge. The OOD, one of the best ship handlers on board and a good friend, ordered our ship all back full to ensure we did not collide. The captain, who had been notified as this situation unfolded, angrily demanded how the OOD and I as the TAO had allowed this to happen.

The captain threw us off the bridge and pulled us off the watch bill—a searing experience made worse by coming at the end of a deployment that had gone so well. I was sure I was finished in this profession, and I'd be lying if I did not admit to having some hard feelings toward the captain, who seemed less interested in why this occurred than that it occurred at all. Remarkably, a number of weeks later, the captain called me in to his cabin for what I expected to be the final nail in the coffin. Instead, he talked about the ultimate accountability he had and that the sea can be an unforgiving place, where bad things can happen to good people in an instant. Although I suspected the captain and I still saw things differently regarding that December morning, I was quietly grateful to receive a second chance. Oddly enough, both the OOD and I would go on to have very successful tours on the ship.

Having now commanded at sea myself as a destroyer captain and commodore, I look back on this incident a bit differently than I did as a young officer at the beginning of my naval service. Frankly, I've led in a different style than that CO, but I also remember those lessons of vigilance and accountability every day. The sea can indeed be a cruel teacher, but I also learned that, in some cases, the beauty of a second chance can make all the difference.

—*RADM Fred Kacher, USN*

PROCEDURES ARE THERE FOR A REASON

During predeployment training of my first SEAL team, a colleague and I were the pilots of a small SEAL submersible. This particular kind of submersible carried four other

SEALs cramped in the water-filled aft compartment. It also carried its own air supply for the passengers in the back, given they were completely separated from the front compartment and seated so tightly together that individual tanks were not possible. We loaded the submersible onto a small commercial ship that would insert us at the first leg of our water infiltration to the shoreline.

The two techs that worked on our submersible wanted to take care of the system checks once we loaded on the commercial ship so we could quickly deploy when we arrived on station. As soon as all the system checks were complete, they shut all of the air valves so there would be no leakage during a multihour transit to the insertion point.

Upon arriving on station, all of the SEALs loaded into the submersible, and we were lifted by crane into the water. Those in the aft compartment tested their breathing hoses from the submersible, and all were okay, giving us the signal to submerge and begin the dive portion of the transit. After about two minutes submerging to our transit depth, we saw the urgent emergency signal from the aft compartment light up, telling us to surface as quickly as possible for an emergency.

What was the emergency? The technicians had forgotten to open the air valves to the aft compartment before we dove. Shutting the air valves for the long transit was a deviation from normal procedures. The dive supervisor did not know these valves had been shut prior to his predive checks and missed their status in his own checks. There was enough residual air in the piping from the secured tanks to give the dive supervisor and SEALs in the back a false positive when they tested the breathing hoses in their own predive checks. Once we dove, all four SEALs immediately ran out of air and were forced to hold their breath for the three minutes to resurface. We were very close to losing four SEALs by not following the procedures as they were written.

The lesson I learned was that procedures, particularly with life-support equipment, are there for a reason—and are often written in blood. A component of competency is not only following procedures but also understanding why they are there in the first place—and recognizing that deviations can kill quickly. This incident taught me to think twice before deviating from any established procedures.

—*CDR Andrew Ledford, USN*

ALL STOP

I failed my first OOD board. It started out well enough. I was breezing through questions about the rules of the road, man-overboard and loss-of-steering situations, the ship's characteristics, and other topics. After about an hour, I was supremely confident that I had impressed my captain and the other OODs enough that my letter was but a congratulatory handshake and signature away. Instead, the captain strategically moved the other OODs around the space—some behind me, some off to the side—simulating the watch stations of a bridge watch team, combat team, and engineering team. He painted an anchoring scenario for me and ordered me to direct the ship to anchorage. No problem. No problem, that is, until things out of my control started going haywire. Contacts being called out from all sides. Hazards to navigation. Potential threats. Do we have a steering casualty? I couldn't get the answers I thought I needed. I drove on. I doubted every order I gave. The sweat was clearly beading on my forehead as I desperately tried to get things right. The more I pressed, the worse it got. Mercifully, the captain called it and told me I needed some more work. I was embarrassed and deflated.

I thought about the scenario the rest of the day and into the evening. At last, I thought I had the answer and went to the captain's cabin. I asked, "Captain, if I had just ordered 'all stop' at some point, would I have passed?" The captain answered, "Exactly. I wasn't going to let you get to that anchorage. All I wanted to know was how long you would risk the safety of my crew and my ship before realizing you needed to slow things down or ask for help."

Lesson learned: There will be occasions when you don't have the solution, and the best course of action then is to buy yourself time to process what's in front of you. There will be times when you take risks and realize that they are not producing the intended results. It's okay to take calculated risks to lead change. When you do, don't ever be afraid to call "all stop" and to consider adjusting your approach. I was fortunate to have a captain savvy enough to impart this wisdom on me in the safety of a simulated anchoring evolution during an OOD board. If he hadn't flushed that ego out of me, I might have actually placed my shipmates' lives and our ship in real peril.

Second lesson learned: I've never taken a new assignment and found that things were absolutely perfect, and I've never read about any navy that achieved supremacy by relying on old ideas, old tactics, old technology, or timid leadership. So don't be afraid to take sensible risks and to implement new ideas. But in doing so, never risk lives unnecessarily, damage equipment, or even sacrifice efficiency because you lack the patience or the humility to order "all stop."

—*CAPT David Rewkowski, USN*

THE BIRD-CAGED WIRE

During one of my first tours on a ship after graduation from a maritime academy, I was in charge of the aft gang as we were preparing to tie up a 50,000-ton oil tanker to an oil platform near the entrance to Drift River, Cook Inlet, Alaska. It was the middle of winter; the temperature was below zero, and the current was roaring through. During that time of year, two pilots maintained a radar watch on the bridge, looking for ice floes that could force us away from the rig and part our lines. During the previous undocking evolution, the mooring wire was improperly stowed on the drum. As we began to pay out the wire, it "bird-caged" on the drum and became wedged within itself. It was dangling in the water. We could no longer pay out or haul in the wire. We tried several times to free it using our usual methods. After several minutes, I radioed up to the captain and told him that we couldn't get it loose. What he said to me was simple yet true, "Mate, you *have* to get it loose."

That line was essential to the safe and effective mooring of the vessel, given the current. There was no workaround. In these conditions, the only way to complete the evolution was to safely free up that wire and make that piece of equipment work. The captain made that perfectly clear to everyone who was listening. After some more time, with some experienced seamen and ingenuity, we freed the wire and were able to tie up properly and safely. This was my first experience being challenged by a problem seemingly so simple, yet so integral to the operation.

Lesson learned: This experience taught me that there is value in every detail of the operation and that sometimes there are problems that need to be solved immediately with a sense of urgency. Sometimes you just have to make it happen, *and* keep everyone safe.

—*Second Mate Aaron Asimakopoulos, Navy Reservist and Merchant Mariner*

THE WARFIGHTER XO

Be professionally competent! Early in my executive officer (XO) tour on an Aegis cruiser, I was up in Combat Information Center (CIC) to observe a combat-systems training scenario. A master chief operations specialist was coordinating it, along with the combat systems officer. The master chief said, "Hey XO, do you want to be TAO for this scenario?" I had been a combat systems officer twice (but not on an Aegis ship), and I had just finished my XO training pipeline. That training included a very good course on the Aegis combat system, including significant time training as a TAO in challenging scenarios. So I felt very confident in my TAO skills and said, "Sure, let's go."

I then ran a very complex, multimission scenario, including control of multiple fighter aircraft against multi-axis attacks. I really felt like I was "in the zone" and orchestrated the entire combat team with crisp orders over our internal net/headphone system. At the end, I called the team together and did a quick debrief of the event. Two nights later, I was on the bridge briefing the CO on eight o'clock reports, and he said, "The master chief was up yesterday and said the ship is abuzz about this new super-warfighter XO that we have." My competency translated to my having great warfighting credibility for the rest of my tour.

Lesson learned: Be professionally competent! If you're going to be a good leader at sea on a complex warship, you have to know your stuff.

—*RADM Kevin Quinn, USN*

FIRST TIME THROUGH THE STRAIT OF MALACCA

I was a brand-new third mate fresh out of the Academy. During my first tour, we were sailing from Seattle to the Far East. Our eastbound route would eventually take us to Singapore and the Strait of Malacca. Just a month prior to our departure, another ship had run hard aground at the entrance to the strait due to navigational error. It happened during the junior third mate's watch. Both the junior third mate and the captain were fired after an inquiry. Before the end of my first day on the ship, our six-foot, six-inch intimidating captain slid a copy of the grounding inquiry under my cabin door. Across the front page he wrote in bold red ink, "THIS WILL NOT HAPPEN ON MY SHIP—BE PREPARED." I began my preparation by praying to God that I would not be on watch when we sailed through the strait!

As the days at sea rolled by, I found myself making one rookie mistake after another and drawing the unwanted attention of the captain and crew. Things were not going well for me; by the time we arrived in Singapore, the captain had little confidence in my ability. After several days of cargo operations in Singapore, I realized to my horror that I would indeed be on watch as we departed Singapore and transited through the Strait of Malacca. After more prayer, I realized that the only way to assure a navigational error-free passage was to literally memorize every navigational light, buoy, number, course, and other information on the chart of the strait. That is exactly what I did. Since the captain had no confidence in me, he informed me that he would be standing my watch with me, observing my navigation while he maintained the conn. The Strait of Malacca is a notoriously dangerous passage highlighted by One Fathom Bank. My effort to memorize all navigational aids, both land and sea, plus courses put me in good shape right up to One Fathom Bank. At that point, something went wrong with my navigation; my plot and fix showed the ship heading far too close to the shoal. With great trepidation I informed the captain. He walked back to the chart, looked down at my work, and snarled at me, "Do it again." By now, the pilot was away, and we were quickly closing on One Fathom Bank. The chart was now a mess, as the sweat from my hands had begun to smear the fixes I was attempting to lay down.

Finally, after being told three times to recheck my fixed bearings and plot, with my stomach churning, I stood squarely in front of the captain and asked him to please take a round of bearings as I could not find my mistake. He was furious but quickly complied in the chart room as I stood next to the helmsmen. That was the longest three minutes of my early career. The captain never came out of the chart room. I heard his booming voice call out: "Third mate, you are correct. Change course to such and such degrees and maintain till the next course change that I have set on the chart. I will be in my cabin if you have any further questions, don't hesitate to call."

To my astonishment, the captain left me on the bridge with the conn. My navigation was correct; we were going to pass dangerously close to One Fathom Bank. My relationship with the captain and crew changed dramatically from that moment on. And I learned one of the greatest lessons of my seagoing career: "Be prepared" through prudent seamanship and constant vigilance.

—*CAPT Grant Livingstone, First Class Pilot,*
Unlimited Tonnage

KNOW YOUR GEAR, AND MAKE IT WORK!

As a lieutenant liaison officer to the Japanese Maritime Self Defense Force, I was assigned to the U.S. Mine Countermeasures Group in the northern Arabian Gulf, then clearing the 1,200 mines that had been laid by the Iraqis. Our ships had found a type of mine that we had never encountered before, and we needed to perform an "exploitation" in order to learn more about this device. The explosive-ordinance disposal (EOD) divers who conducted this evolution—never done before on a live weapon—used their normal procedures. This included attaching lifting bags that fill with air to raise the mine so it can be beached for full investigation. This was a large weapon, so large that when the lifting bags were filled and the mine started to rise, the bags broke and the mine settled back on the bottom.

With no options, I set my mind to figuring out a way to make this happen. I was very familiar with all the various equipment at our disposal. Determining that we needed more lifting power, plus the ability to rig the device for towing, I proposed that we use the O, or Oropesa, floats. These are normally used for towing mechanical minesweeping gear through the water. Since the lifting bags could get the mine off the bottom but not hold it or make it towable, I suggested that the EOD divers lift the mine with the bags and then transfer the rig to the O floats, which were much more stable and reliable. It worked!

Lesson learned: As a young officer, know your gear, be resourceful, and make suggestions supported by the competency you have earned. Technical savvy and ingenuity will make you stand out as a leader.

—*CAPT Arthur Stauff, USN*

THE TWO-DAY LEADERSHIP LESSON

I was a young, twenty-six-year-old lieutenant (jg), newly assigned as damage control assistant on a nuclear attack submarine. We were conducting one of those "special operations of great importance to the defense of the United States," which is a fancy way of saying we were on an important mission where (a) we had to have continuous submarine coverage, (b) we could not transmit, and (c) if we were forced to leave station, another submarine would be sent in to replace us. And as usually happens during a mission of such duration, "Murphy" raised his head. This time it was in the form of a leak in the ship's service hydraulic power plant accumulator—a large and complex piece of equipment that usually was repaired by an intermediate maintenance activity (IMA), not the ship's crew.

Fortunately, my leading petty officer (LPO) had served shore duty in an IMA and had conducted several similar repairs. After analyzing the failure with him, I went forward to give the captain the good news and the bad news. The bad news: the accumulator would have to be taken off service for several hours, if not days. The good news: we were fairly confident we could actually repair it at sea—we would not have to leave station. The captain gave us permission to start the repair.

The disassembly effort took the better part of a day, and my LPO remained on station supervising during the entire affair. All my Sailors vowed to stay awake until the job was done, and thinking this would be a good learning experience for them, I let them.

Finally, after about thirty hours of continuous work without sleep, eating in shifts, and taking short breaks when we could, the accumulator was reassembled, and it was time to leak-check the device. We pressurized it, and *wham!*— it leaked worse than before. My division's disappointment was understandable but was magnified a hundredfold by the extreme fatigue brought on by over a day of continuous work. Now the problem was worse than before, and my guys were too exhausted to do anything about it. This was without a doubt the hardest report I had ever brought to my captain in my still-new submarine career. My own sense of personal guilt was nearly intolerable. So while my guys were sleeping, I went over the system drawings again to see if I could figure out what went wrong. Then I remembered something I had heard months before—the engineering yeoman who maintains the ship's drawings was way behind in updating our files. So on a hunch, I went to the ship's microfiche index to see what version of the drawings we should have been using. Sure enough, I discovered that the plans we were using during the repair had been superseded. When I printed out the new drawings, it turned out it had leaked because we installed the wrong part. Should my LPO have figured this out before we started the repairs? Of course. But I was the division officer, and it was my responsibility. While my zeal to exhibit "deckplate leadership" was appropriate (and would continue to serve me well in later years), it did not absolve me of my responsibility as the division officer.

What did I learn? While I was "hanging" with my guys, no one was doing that "officer stuff" I should have been doing—checking to ensure that we were using the right drawings and procedures, that the right parts were being used, that proper precautions were being followed, and that the job would get done right. It was my fault the final repair would be delayed by more than two days. This was a lesson I would never forget.

—*CAPT William Toti, USN*

BE A PERPETUAL STUDENT

I am both a naval officer and a U.S. Merchant Marine master mariner. Working in both capacities has allowed me to learn to be a good seaman. The Army teaches its officers to be soldiers first; similarly, naval officers should be seamen first. When assigned to a ship as an officer, learn to be a seaman first—and always take the initiative to learn—because every day on board ship is different, and the development of professional competency will always serve you well.

One lesson learned: Don't take the quartermaster's word regarding where the ship is. Instead, learn to navigate. Don't take the weather report for granted. Instead, learn weather and how to interpret changing conditions. In fact, learn about everything that occurs in your surroundings, because doing so creates optimal situational awareness. Learning as much as possible makes you a better seaman and, therefore, a better officer.

At a basic level, this is leadership by example. Sailors respect a real seaman and recognize competency. I'm a harbor pilot by specialty now, and I also dock ships for the Navy as a reserve officer. While confiding in a senior pilot one day about the challenges of piloting in my waters, he pointedly told me, "Be confident in your knowledge." His guidance was true and succinct. And it reminded me that professional competency is an ongoing investment in one's career. To be good and safe at your job, you must be a perpetual student.

—CAPT Alexander Soukhanov, USN

CHAPTER 9

LEADERSHIP ADVICE FROM
THOSE WHO HAVE LED

While I recommend in the strongest terms to the respective officers, activity, vigilance, and firmness—, I feel no less solicitude that their deportment may be marked with prudence, moderation, and good temper.

Always keep in mind that [your] country-men are free men, and as such, are impatient of everything that bears the least mark of a domi-neering spirit. . . . [T]herefore, refrain, with the most guarded circumspection, from whatever has the semblance of haughtiness, rudeness, or insult. . . .

. . . [E]ndeavor to overcome difficulties, if any are experienced, by a cool and temperate perseverance in . . . duty—by address and mod-eration, rather than by vehemence and violence.

—*ALEXANDER HAMILTON*

In chapter 3, in an attempt to "define" leadership, we provided a few of the leadership lists resident in thirty-five of the thousands of books written on the subject. When we looked at those lists, we saw some characteristics that were repeated again and again. You'll notice that these lists include what a leader should *be* (traits), and what a leader should be *capable of* (skills or competencies).

In chapters 4–8, we provided sea stories that illustrate some of those traits and skills. In this chapter, we move away from lists of traits and sea stories. Here, we'll give you straightforward advice from those who've led those like you, leaders in the sea services.

First, we surveyed hundreds of sea-service officers, compiling the findings of their responses here. In the dozens of leadership lists you've seen in this book, this is the newest! Second, we researched institutional sources to gather the advice others have provided on what you should do to be a leader.

THE SEA-SERVICE SURVEY

We invited members of the sea services (Navy, Marine Corps, Coast Guard, and Merchant Marine) to give us their view on the "primary traits required of a successful junior officer."

We asked them to choose from a list of seventy-six potential positive traits, which are listed in alphabetical order in the following table. Each was asked to select up to eight of these traits they considered as most important for effective leadership and eight traits they valued but found of lesser importance.

Approximately 380 people responded to the survey. They represented, cumulatively, nearly nine thousand years of experience, or an average of about twenty-four years per respondent. Male and female officers responded, both active and retired. They ranged in rank from E-7 (senior enlisted) to O-9 (vice admiral) in the military services, and from third mate to master/chief engineer in the Merchant Marine.

Seventy-Six Potential Positive Traits in a Junior Officer

Ability to Build Teams	Foresight	Positive Attitude
Accountability	Imagination	Professionalism
Adaptability	Initiative	Prudence
Agreeableness	Innovation, Creativity	Resourcefulness
Ambition	Inquisitiveness	Responsiveness
Analytical Thinking	Insight	Scholarship
Attention to Detail	Inspiration	Self-Control
Boldness/Daring	Instinct	Selflessnes
Caution	Integrity, Honor	Sense of Humor
Character, Strength of	Intellect	Sensitivity
Commitment	Interpersonal Sensitivity	Sociability
Conscience	Intuition	Speaking Ability
Conscientiousness	Judgment	Spirituality
Conviction	Leadership Presence	Tactical Proficiency
Decisiveness	Loyalty	Teamwork
Dedication	Maturity	Technical Competence
Dependability	Military Bearing	Tenacity
Determination	Moral Courage	Tidiness
Diligence	Optimism	Trustworthiness
Discipline	Passion	Versatility
Drive	Patience	Vigor
Emotional Intelligence	Perseverance	Vision
Empathy	Physical Courage	Work Ethic
Endurance	Physical Fitness	Writing Ability
Enthusiasm	Politeness	
Focus	Political Awareness	

The votes of each respondent were weighted, with "primary" traits being scored at twice the value of a "secondary" one, to form a total score for each trait. The most desired traits, and those least selected, are listed on page 158.

Now, these lists are very interesting and provide some useful results. But the review of seventy-six individual words in a single list of traits might lead to some erroneous conclusions.

Top Ten Desired Traits		Least Desired Traits	
Trait	**Score**	**Trait**	**Score**
Integrity, Honor	465	Sensitivity	7
Character, Strength of	354	Scholarship	7
Trustworthiness	317	Tidiness	8
Judgment	316	Political Awareness	11
Accountability	314	Politeness	12
Work Ethic	311	Spirituality	14
Dependability	310	Prudence	17
Initiative	302	Vigor	18
Positive Attitude	290	Agreeableness	19
Professionalism	253	Insight	23

What if we grouped the seventy-six traits into a smaller set of more general categories?

Many of the seventy-six traits are related—they refer to a common, more general attribute. For instance, "integrity" and "character" are very similar and could be grouped together. When we analyzed the individual traits, they seemed to naturally cluster into seven larger groups, as shown on page 159.

It's interesting to see how the 380 senior sea-going leaders emphasized these seven potential trait groups. To do that, we analyzed and normalized the responses across those groups to account for the varying number of traits in each. The following table shows the emphasis these leaders collectively placed on the seven larger areas.

As you can see, they emphasized character and integrity issues above all else. Next, they wanted a professional teammate—a good shipmate. Third, they valued initiative and a strong work ethic. The bottom line results are clear, perhaps self-evident.

Seventy-Six Traits Sorted into Groups

WORK ETHIC/INITIATIVE	CHARACTER & INTEGRITY	SKILLS
Ambition	Accountability	Attention to Detail
Boldness/Daring	Character, Strength of	Military Bearing
Caution	Conscience	Patience
Commitment	Conscientiousness	Physical Fitness
Decisiveness	Conviction	Politeness
Dedication	Dependability	Speaking Ability
Determination	Discipline	Tactical Proficiency
Diligence	Integrity, Honor	Technical Competence
Drive	Moral Courage	Tidiness
Endurance	Physical Courage	Writing Ability
Enthusiasm	Self-Control	
Focus	Trustworthiness	**JUDGMENT & MATURITY**
Imagination		
Initiative	**PERSONALITY**	Foresight
Passion		Insight
Perseverance	Adaptability	Instinct
Positive Attitude	Agreeableness	Intuition
Prudence	Emotional Intelligence	Judgment
Resourcefulness	Interpersonal Sensitivity	Maturity
Responsiveness	Optimism	Vision
Tenacity	Political Awareness	
Versatility	Sense of Humor	**TEAMING & LEADERSHIP**
Vigor	Sensitivity	
Work Ethic	Sociability	Ability to Build Teams
	Spirituality	Inspiration
INTELLECT		Leadership Presence
		Loyalty
Analytical Thinking		Professionalism
Innovation, Creativity		Selflessness
Inquisitiveness		Teamwork
Intellect		
Scholarship		

Results of Survey by Group

Trait Group	Score
Character Integrity	203
Teaming	155
Work Ethic Initiative	109
Skills	99
Judgment Maturity	92
Intellect	83
Personality	62

The 380 responding sea-going leaders, representing years of experience, placed 6,000 votes against a tally of 76 potential leadership traits they wanted to see in a junior officer assigned to their ship.

And what did they want? Character and integrity (honesty). A good shipmate who can work as part of a larger team (teammate). A hard worker with a good attitude and the initiative to get things done (hard-working). In short, they wanted an *honest, hard-working teammate.*

They felt that skills could be taught and that judgment and maturity would come in time. They felt that personality wasn't as important. (But before you assume that an unpleasant shipboard personality is acceptable, remember that there is a healthy dose of "personality" embedded in the ability to work well on teams, which they highly valued.)

So there it is—the results of the survey. The bottom line of the latest leadership list: According to the collective advice of hundreds of senior sea-service leaders, to be a successful leader, you should work to be an—

Honest, Hard-Working Teammate.

ADVICE FROM OTHER AUTHORITATIVE SOURCES

Now that we've explained what our 380 officers said about being an honest, hard-working teammate, let's look at some lists of advice from military, business, and academic sources.

The *Division Officer's Guide* provides a wonderful and straightforward list called "Principles of Naval Leadership":

- Know your job
- Know yourself

- Know and take care of your subordinates
- Set a positive example
- Project a clear vision and communicate effectively
- Direct, motivate, and develop subordinates
- Demonstrate effective management skills
- Build effective teams

That's a great, classic list. Any young officer should post it above his or her desk.

ADM Kinnard McKee was once the superintendent at the Naval Academy and later the head of the Navy's Nuclear Power Program. Many years ago, when we were young officers, he told us that we should strive as follows: Know your job. Know your people. Know yourself. That simple advice resonates with us today.

Each year, the Navy's Center for Personal and Professional Development publishes the *Navy Leader Planning Guide*, which contains calendars, references, historic information, checklists, phone numbers, and other data vital to young leaders.

Among many other interesting lists, it provides the "11 Principles of Naval Leadership":

1. Know yourself and seek self-improvement.
2. Be technically and tactically proficient.
3. Know your subordinates and look out for their welfare.
4. Keep your subordinates informed.
5. Set the example.
6. Ensure the task is understood, supervised, and accomplished.
7. Train your unit as a team.

8. Make sound and timely decisions.
9. Develop a sense of responsibility among your subordinates.
10. Employ your command in accordance with its capabilities.
11. Seek responsibility and take responsibility for your actions.

For nearly 110 years, *The Bluejacket's Manual* has guided Sailors with advice and wisdom. The centennial edition of this classic, written by LCDR Thomas Cutler, USN (Ret.), offers the following ten pieces of leadership advice:

1. Reverse roles (consider the Golden Rule).
2. Take responsibility.
3. Set the example.
4. Praise in public; correct in private.
5. Be consistent, but not inflexible.
6. Know your job.
7. Do not micromanage.
8. Practice good followership.
9. Don't be one of the gang.
10. Keep your subordinates informed.

Michael Abrashoff was commanding officer of the Aegis guided missile destroyer USS *Benfold* (DDG 65). After his successful tour as CO, he wrote the book *It's Your Ship*, which is now used as a leadership text at some maritime academies. He provides eleven major pieces of advice:

1. Take command.
2. Lead by example.
3. Listen aggressively.

4. Communicate purpose and meaning.
5. Create a climate of trust.
6. Look for results, not salutes.
7. Take calculated risks.
8. Go beyond standard procedure.
9. Build up your people.
10. Generate unity.
11. Improve your people's quality of life.

As CDR Abrashoff learned leadership lessons while serving as a leader, so too did MAJ John Chapman, USA. He wrote up his lessons learned in the book *Muddy Boots Leadership*. He concludes with his "Ten Rules to Live by for Leaders":

1. Be at the critical time and place—every day has (at least) one.
2. Everything in life is a graded event.
3. Common sense counts.
4. Discipline begins with self-discipline.
5. Wear your heart on your sleeve; your soldiers must know how you feel.
6. Subordinates learn by your example, whether you intend it or not.
7. Five minutes' checking on the guards in a freezing rain at midnight is worth a year of payday speeches.
8. Considering input doesn't make you weak; it makes you smart.
9. You gain authority by giving it.
10. What you see is as important as what you choose not to see.

In a similar way, but in a more institutional sense, the Marine Corps has memorialized its view of proper leadership in *Leading Marines* (Field Manual FMFM 1-0). It lists eleven pieces of advice to become a leader of Marines:

1. Be technically and tactically proficient.
2. Know yourself and seek self-improvement.
3. Know your Marines and look out for their welfare.
4. Keep your Marines informed.
5. Set the example.
6. Ensure the task is understood, supervised, and accomplished.
7. Train your Marines as a team.
8. Make sound and timely decisions.
9. Develop a sense of responsibility among your subordinates.
10. Employ your unit in accordance with its capabilities.
11. Seek responsibility, and take responsibility for your actions.

Speaking of Marine Corps leadership, two former Marines left the military, went into the business world, and later wrote *Semper Fi: Business Leadership the Marine Corps Way*. In the book's section on "Leading the Rank and File," they described eighteen leadership commandments for achieving excellence:

1. Create a culture that exalts the workforce.
2. Inspire through personal example.
3. Understand that the employee who feels cared for will care about the company.

4. Combine fire-breathing enthusiasm with solicitous mentoring.
5. Empower those closest to the task to make decisions.
6. Expand departmental pride into a corporate-wide phenomenon.
7. Institutionalize the supervisor as the corporate teacher.
8. Recognize followership as the precursor to leadership.
9. Convert personal ambition into commitment to the corporate mission.
10. Implement a "manager's school" for all levels of management.
11. Require and support continuing education.
12. Empower and delegate, but be available to your subordinates.
13. Expect all associates to keep pace with the strides of the organization.
14. Implement company-wide "subject readiness" tests.
15. Promote constructive competition.
16. Provide all associates with a communications path all the way to the top.
17. Reach out to the families of the workforce and managerial staff.
18. Exalt seniority, while maintaining performance expectations.

Dale Carnegie was the businessman who wrote the classic *How to Win Friends and Influence People*. (If you haven't read it, find a copy and read it today!) His company,

Dale Carnegie Training, produced the book *Leadership Mastery: How to Challenge Yourself and Others to Greatness*. It provides advice in the form of a list of "practical tactics and techniques":

1. Master the decision-making process.
2. Clearly articulate expectations.
3. Only make promises that you can keep.
4. Use humor whenever possible.
5. Be respected *and* liked.
6. Master one-on-one communication.
7. Be consistent.
8. Understand the four stages of competency.[1]
9. Always respond within 24 hours.

A far more nuanced view of the complexities of leadership is provided in *The Contrarian's Guide to Leadership*, by Stephen Sample. The author uses his book to teach a set of nine lessons for the leader who is maturing beyond basic leadership skills.

1. Think "gray." Become comfortable in the gray area between black and white. Don't get carried away categorizing things as good or bad, true or false, friend or foe.

---

[1] The first stage is unconscious incompetence; you're no good, and you don't know it. The second stage is conscious incompetence; you're still no good, but at least you recognize that fact. The third stage is conscious competence; you're good, you're skilled, but you have to think about it to be that way. The fourth and highest stage is unconscious competence; you're really good, and you don't have to think about it—it becomes natural.

2. Listen artfully. Use listening to acquire new ideas and gather new information.

3. Experts can be saviors, and they can be charlatans. Be careful, and be able to distinguish what kind of expert you're dealing with.

4. You are what you read. Read the right things!

5. Two rules on decisions. First, never make a decision yourself that can reasonably be delegated to a subordinate. Second, never make a decision today that can reasonably be put off to tomorrow.

6. Know which hill you're willing to die on.

7. Work for those who work for you.

8. Follow the leader. Leaders create followers.

9. Don't just be the leader; *do* the leader. Do the hard things you must do to fulfill the role of leader. Leadership isn't a state of "being"—it is a state of "doing."

We encourage you to reread this list and focus on lesson four!

Peter Drucker is the grandfather of management and leadership study. His classic book is *The Effective Executive: The Definitive Guide to Getting the Right Things Done*. In it, he identifies eight practices of successful executives.

1. They asked: "What needs to be done?"

2. They asked: "What is right for the enterprise?"

3. They developed action plans.

4. They took responsibility for decisions.

5. They took responsibility for communications.

6. They were focused on opportunities rather than problems.

7. They ran productive meetings.
8. They thought and said "we" rather than "I."

This is a formidable list—in eight short practices, it encapsulates the essence of the effective leader. You can turn each of these "practices" into a simple piece of advice. For instance, Drucker observes that good leaders run productive meetings. So his advice is: "Learn how to run productive meetings!"

Finally, just as we saw Churchill's views on competencies, we can refer to *Churchill on Leadership* to get some leadership advice from that great leader. His guidelines on personnel and administration:

- Establish trust in your subordinates.
- Give clear direction.
- Back up your people through thick and thin.
- Keep fully informed; get your information directly from the source.
- Stick to priorities.
- Have a consistent method and discipline.

His thought process for leaders:

- Always concentrate on the broad view and the central features of the problem at hand.
- Factor in risk and chance by keeping things in proper proportion.
- Keep open to changing your mind in the presence of new facts.
- Be careful not to look too far ahead.
- Avoid excessive perfectionism.
- Don't make decisions for decision's sake.

One final set of advice is provided in the business book *The Leadership Challenge: How to Keep Getting Extraordinary Things Done in Organizations.* The authors suggest five fundamental pieces of advice to achieve exemplary leadership, each of which has two primary components.

1. *Challenge the Process.* Leaders venture out. They are pioneers.

   a) Search out challenging opportunities to change, grow, innovate, and improve.

   b) Experiment, take risks, and learn from the accompanying mistakes.

2. *Inspire a Shared Vision.* Leaders breathe life into the hopes and dreams of others and enable them to see the exciting possibilities that the future holds.

   a) Envision an uplifting and ennobling future.

   b) Enlist others in a common vision by appealing to their values, interests, hopes, and dreams.

3. *Enable Others to Act.* Leaders enlist the support and assistance of all those who must make the project work. They enable others through trust.

   a) Foster collaboration by promoting cooperative goals and building trust.

   b) Strengthen people by giving power away, providing choice, developing competence, assigning critical tasks, and offering visible support.

4. *Model the Way.* Leaders model through personal example and dedicated execution.

   a) Set the example by behaving in ways that are consistent with shared values.

   b) Achieve small wins that promote consistent progress and build commitment.

5. *Encourage the Heart.* Leaders encourage the hearts of their constituents to carry on.

   a) Recognize individual contributions to the success of every project.

   b) Celebrate team accomplishments regularly.

CHAPTER 10

BECOMING THE LEADER
YOU WANT TO BE

⚓

The greatest problem facing the career naval officer is leadership. Yet this most important factor
in an [officer's] life frequently is allowed to grow
like a choice flower in a garden surrounded by
rank weeds.

So many feel that if they follow the average
course of naval life, experience will finally give
them the qualities of a great leader.... Few realize
that the growth to sound leadership is a life's work.

Ambition alone will not encompass it. ...
The path to qualification for leadership [at sea]
is a long, hard road to travel. It is a path of life.

—*ADM WILLIAM V. PRATT*

Let's return to the two points made in previous chapters. First, you can become the leader you want to
be. Second, it's not rocket science. You can acquire
leadership skills if you choose to. Remember SPOM: *Study,
Practice, Observation, Mentorship.* You are now, officially,
as you read these words, at a junction point in your life.
You can go two ways.

You can be one of the 90 percent of junior officers who
will read these words, put this book down, and probably
never think about it again.

> You've got to be careful if you don't know where you're going, because you might not get there.
>
> —*Yogi Berra*

Or you can be one of the 10 percent who resolves to create a plan to be all the leader that you can be. If you're one of the 90 percent, I hope this book was helpful in some way, and I hope you'll put it on your bookshelf for future reference. Good luck in the fleet! If you're one of the 10 percent, or are considering being in that select group, read on for these last few pages.

BECOMING THE LEADER YOU WANT TO BE

Hopefully by now you're convinced that leadership is important—important to your team, your career, and your service. Ultimately, your leadership is important to your nation. If you want to be a better leader, then there are three simple steps to take.

Step One: Decide What Leadership Means to You

Decide on your own definition of the leader you want to be. What is *your* definition, *your* list of traits and attributes and skills and practices? Don't make it too lengthy. We recommend against the "100 attributes of a leader" school. Instead, think of ten or a dozen things that are important to you, perhaps in categories, or buckets.

Here's one example of a leadership model: ENS Kathy Sullivan on a Navy destroyer believes that leadership is about two buckets: *traits* and *skills*. She has drawn up her list of her five most important *traits* and seven most valued *skills* into the following matrix:

ENS Sullivan's Personal Leadership Model	
TRAITS	**SKILLS**
Honesty	Communication
Compassion	Delegation
Work Ethic	Listening
Loyalty	Team-Building
Sense of Humor	Inciting Fun
	Planning
	Caring for People

This is Kathy's own personal leadership model. A model doesn't have to be fancy. But it does have to be personal. What works for others won't necessarily work for you.

Here's another example: LTJG Mike Herbert is a Coast Guard helicopter pilot. He's most comfortable with the Be-Know-Do model of leadership as described in chapter 3. The buckets on his personal leadership list are threefold: who you are (Be), your skillsets (Know), and your actions (Do). For him, each bucket has four items to remember. He likes this model because he can recite it using the fingers of one hand, and the three buckets, with four items each, equal a perfect dozen.

LTJG Herbert's Personal Leadership Model		
BE	**KNOW**	**DO**
Who You Are	*Your skillsets*	*Your actions*
Courageous	Great ship-driver	Set goals
A Team Player	Excellent navigator	Drive hard
Honest	Delegation	Care for the troops
Loyal	Communication	Get the job done

Mike's model is different from Kathy's, but it doesn't matter because it works for him. The important thing is to have your own model. It doesn't have to last a lifetime—it'll change, we promise. But if you want to be a leader, you need to decide for yourself what being a leader is.

In the space to the right, take ten minutes and write down what *your* personal leadership model might look like. Pick from one to four buckets. Pick from one to seven items per bucket. Fill it in. Try it out!

Now that you've built your own leadership model, let's move to the next step.

Step Two: Determine Where You Need Improvement

Once you have a rough picture of what you think a leader should be, it's time to assess yourself to find where you need improvement. To use business-speak jargon, it's time for a "gap analysis" between the "as is" (what you are today) and the "to be" (what you want to be tomorrow). How can you determine where you need improvement?

The first is self-assessment. You'll probably have some innate sense of what you're good at and where you're weak. Do an honest, gut-feel assessment of where you stand against each of your desired traits and skills. Are you honest? Do you really care about your folks? Are you good at delegating, or are you a micromanager? Are you willing to give recognition to others, even when it means people don't know how well you did personally?

The second assessment method is through mentoring and advice from friends. Find a confidant—a peer or a senior whom you trust—and ask them: "How am I at delegating? How strong or weak am I at X, Y, and Z? If I had to improve

Your Leadership Model
(Fill in the buckets and items in each bucket.)

Bucket				
1				
2				
3				
4				
5				
6				
7				

in three areas, what would they be?" Most people will push back and will be reluctant to offer you constructive criticism for fear they'll lose you as a friend. Get past this. The best thing they can do is give you the feedback you need. We've found that when we ask people (seniors or peers) to give three palpable suggestions for improvement, they'll eventually cough them up—if we are adamant about it.

By the way, when they do finally offer some suggestions, don't be defensive! Don't argue! Don't attack them! Just be grateful, and thank them.

The third method of self-analysis is through 360-degree feedback. In this case, you ask your peers, your seniors, and your subordinates to grade you on your leadership traits and skills. You can make up a survey, or you can go on the Internet to purchase a service to provide it. These surveys are confidential, and if properly administered, they're the best way to get unfiltered feedback. They're the most work to make happen but will provide the best information for your game plan. In the Navy, as well as in many Fortune 500 companies, senior officers are given formal 360-degree feedback to help them get an unvarnished view on how they can be better.

Let's say you've identified ten leadership skills you feel are part of the leader you want to be. Your goal is to decide where you're average, where you're strong, and where you're weak. Those three levels of skills are sufficient. Your initial game plan will be to work on your weak areas.

Step Three: Fix It through a Long-Term SPOM Game Plan
Once you've identified where you need some improvement, it's time to build a brief SPOM game plan. Remember,

SPOM is Study, Practice, Observation, and Mentorship. The plan doesn't have to be voluminous or overwhelming. Let's say you've decided that one of your weaknesses as a leader is your difficulty in establishing personal connections with your people.

Your plan to work on that could be as simple as the following:

Study: Read a book on personal connections, such as *Emotional Intelligence* by Daniel Goleman or *How to Win Friends and Influence People* by Dale Carnegie. Theodore Roosevelt, who was a voracious reader, said, "I am a part of everything I have read." Conversely, everything you read becomes a part of you! Your reading is a diet for your brain; pick the right nourishment.

Practice: Once a month, invite one of the members of your team to lunch and talk about his or her issues and concerns and needs and plans. Practice using the techniques and tips you read about.

Observation: Watch and learn from an experienced officer who seems to be a whiz at connecting with people and understanding where they are and what they need. How does that officer do that?

Mentorship: Visit with your commanding officer twice a year and ask for advice on how to be better at making connections. Ask for feedback from your commander's perspective.

That's it. Again, this doesn't have to be complicated. No calculus involved. It doesn't take a PhD. It simply takes you identifying some weakness, some area in which you want to improve, and using the moments of time it takes to get better in that area.

Anyone who stops learning is old, whether at twenty
or eighty. Anyone who keeps learning stays young. The
greatest thing in life is to keep your mind young.

—Henry Ford

If you were a high-school basketball player and were great at running and dribbling and shooting from inside but couldn't hit a free throw to save your life, what would you do? You'd study free throws. You'd practice shooting free throws. You'd observe players who were good free-throw shooters. And you'd get your coaches to show you how to improve your free-throw technique. And, as a result, you'd become a better free-throw shooter and a better player overall.

So it is with your leadership skills. Only, in the vast scheme of things, sea-service leadership skills are so very, very much more important than high school basketball skills. They deserve that much more attention.

Be like Ben Franklin

Remember Benjamin Franklin? He was a writer, printer, businessman, inventor, statesman, and diplomat. A renaissance man among renaissance men, he was one of the most talented and gifted Americans who has ever lived. Ben wasn't necessarily *born* as talented as he was known for being later in life—he *became* that way. Did you know that Ben had his own version of the three-step improvement method described above?

In his *Autobiography,* Ben writes about how he was intent on bettering himself. He admitted being committed to "the bold and arduous project of arriving at Moral

Perfection." He created his own list of thirteen virtues: Temperance, Silence, Order, Resolution, Frugality, Industry, Sincerity, Justice, Moderation, Cleanliness, Tranquility, Chastity, and Humility. Each week he concentrated on a single virtue, so that in the course of fifty-two weeks, he'd go through the list four times. He kept a notebook in which, each week, he would write down his successes and failures. Ben studied the virtues; he practiced them; he observed them in others; he sought advice from others. He identified where he wanted to be stronger, and he employed a SPOM methodology to become better. It was good enough for Ben. It should be good enough for you, too!

A Sample One-Page Plan

Let's look at a simple example of a junior-officer improvement program. Say ENS Kathy Sullivan, in the previous example, has listed her desired traits and skills and has done some analysis and soul-searching to see how she stacks up against her model of a young leader. The preliminary results are:

Sample One-Page Plan			
	Attribute	**Comparison to Goal**	**Action Plan**
TRAITS	Honesty	*Great! Above avg.*	
	Compassion	*Average*	
	Work Ethic	*Slightly weak*	*Need work*
	Loyalty	*Above avg.—strong*	
	Sense of Humor	*Below average!*	*Need work*
SKILL SETS	Communication	*Slightly below avg.*	*Need work*
	Delegation	*Terrible. I stink here!*	*Need lots of work!*
	Listening	*Good at this...*	
	Team-Building	*Good here*	
	Inciting Fun	*Great! Above avg.*	
	Planning	*Below average*	*Need work*
	Caring for People	*Good here*	

As you can see, it doesn't have to be lengthy or complicated. Just decide where you want to be better. In this case, Kathy has decided that of her twelve leadership traits and skills, she needs work on five of them. Once you've identified where you need work, then decide what to do. How can one improve?

Read a book. Listen to a CD or podcast. Scan the Internet. Talk to a mentor. Take a class. Ask a friend for advice. Ask your boss for advice. Whatever you do, come up with your own action plan.

Here's Kathy's example:

Sample One-Page Plan

	Attribute	Comparison to Goal	Action Plan
TRAITS	Honesty	Great! Above avg.	
	Compassion	Average	
	Work Ethic	Slightly weak	Talk to the Skipper; start work 30 min. earlier each day
	Loyalty	Above avg.—strong	
	Sense of Humor	Below average!	Go to jokes.com; memorize ten jokes; practice one/week!
SKILL SETS	Communication	Slightly below avg.	Read the book: Give Your Speech, Change the World
	Delegation	Terrible. I stink here!	Listen to the "One Minute Manager" podcast
	Listening	Good at this...	
	Team-Building	Good here	
	Inciting Fun	Great! Above avg.	
	Planning	Below average	Go to the one-day planning course the Ops Boss told me about...
	Caring for People	Good here	

When you're done with those areas, think of other actions that can make you better. As you progress as a leader, you'll find other weaknesses you'll want to work on. The exercise above is not a one-time event—it's something you do again and again. It's a habit that will get you where you want to go.

> The greatest discovery of my generation is that human beings can alter their lives by altering their attitude of mind.
>
> —William James, Psychologist

Now, dear seagoing-officer readers, you're sophisticated, you're smart, and you're savvy. The above exercise perhaps seems too silly, too simple to be useful. "Write down what I want to improve in?" you ask. Seems hardly worth the time.

That's where you're wrong. Experience shows that someone who writes something down, however simple, is more likely to get it done. If a person determines in his head that he wants to lose fifteen pounds, his chances of actually losing it go up dramatically if he writes it down and posts that note where he can see it daily. Sounds unbelievable, but it's fact. There is power in the declaration in writing, even if the writing is only a note to yourself.

A Proposed Leadership Model for You, the Young Officer at Sea

We've reviewed multiple models, and I've asked you to pick one or invent one. Before you do, here's a potential model just for you. It's based on the cumulative results of this book. For ease of memory, think of a star, or think of the memory aid "TEAMS." Most of your junior-officer leadership will involve leading a team—a shipboard division, a platoon, a squadron department, a technical group, a boat crew.

For you, the young officer, your leadership model can be broken into the five points of a star, the first initials of which make the word TEAMS.

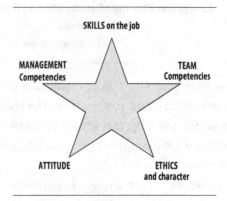

The Five Pillars of TEAMS

The five pillars of this potential leadership model:

T: *Team* competencies
- project management
- team building skills
- ability to get along with others
- followership

E: *Ethics* and character
- honesty and integrity
- dependability
- trustworthiness

A: *Attitude*
- work ethic
- optimism
- discipline
- initiative
- perseverance

M: *Management* competencies
- delegation
- receiving (listening)
- transmitting (spoken and written)

S: *Skills* on the job
- professional competence
- knowledge

This is just one more model for you to consider. If you want to use this model, and choose to implement a SPOM action plan, here is a sample action plan for you:

Regardless of what model you choose—regardless of what kind of action plan you write—take an hour of your busy life and make a plan for the rest of your life. As the Chinese proverb goes, "The journey of a thousand miles begins with a single step." Or, as some of my seagoing friends have (correctly) noted, "A failure to plan is a plan to fail." You've already set yourself apart by reading this far in the book. So continue that with this last and final step—your own personal action plan for growing as a leader.

Most of you won't do it, unfortunately. But if you want to be in that top 10 percent, or in that top 1 percent considered the best of the best, you *must* do things that most

Your Action Plan
(Fill in how you assess your own levels and steps to improve.)

Leadership Area	My Assessment	Steps to Improve
T: TEAM competencies		
Project Management		
Team Building		
Getting Along with Others		
Followership		
E: ETHICS and Character		
Honesty and Integrity		
Dependability		
Trustworthiness		
A: ATTITUDE		
Work Ethic		
Optimism		
Discipline		
Initiative		
Perseverance		
M: MANAGEMENT Competencies		
Delegation		
Receiving (Listening)		
Transmitting (Speaking and Writing)		
S: SKILLS on the Job		
Professional Competence		
Knowledge		

people don't do. Planning, studying, and taking prepared action is part of it. A half hour a week to improve your leadership skills will very soon set you apart.

Theodore Roosevelt was a sickly child. Through will and tenacity, he made himself into the "rough rider" and outdoorsman history knows. He eventually led troops in the Spanish-American War, he helped lead our Navy as Assistant Secretary of the Navy, and eventually he led our country as president. Roosevelt said, "With self-discipline, most anything is possible." He overcame much with self-discipline. Self-discipline can make you the leader you want to be. All you have to do is overcome the inertia of the next hour. If you want it, you can do it.

CLOSING

So there you go. We looked briefly at the six basic questions on leadership. We reviewed ten thousand pages of books, which cumulatively demonstrated common themes of what it means to be a leader—common attributes, common skillsets, common actions and habits.

We reviewed dozens of sea stories and bits of leadership advice from those same stories because, as you'll remind yourself, parables are a great way to learn lessons. And, in the school of hard knocks, if you can learn from someone else's knocks, so much the better!

We polled 380 senior seagoing leaders on what they think is most important in a young seagoing officer like you. They valued integrity and character above all else. But when their six thousand votes and nine thousand years of experience were boiled down to their essence, what they really wanted in a young new officer on their ship was an *Honest, Hard-Working Teammate.*

We reviewed leadership advice from those who know. And, finally, we looked in this chapter at how a young sea-going officer like you might begin to follow in the footsteps of other great leaders who started out just like you: new, learning, trying to understand the art and the science of getting others to do what you want them to do—the things in life that need to be done, but won't get done without the catalyst of leadership.

We hope that you take to heart the three truths that we discussed in the first chapter:

1. Leadership is important.
2. Leadership can be defined and described.
3. Leadership can be learned.

Leadership is, indeed, important. Arguably, it is the most salient and necessary part of your sea-service career. It's definable, even though definitions vary according to the leader and the circumstance. And, most vital to you, it can be learned.

You *can* be the leader you want to be—the leader your service needs you to be—the leader your people and your shipmates need you to be; perhaps, even, the leader your country needs you to be.

We hope that this book has helped you cast off the lines as you depart on your voyage toward being a leader. May your course prove straight and true and that you reach your intended destination. Fair winds and following seas!

THE THIRTY-FIVE LEADERSHIP BOOKS

The Sea Service Books

The Bluejacket's Manual, 25th Edition
> Thomas J. Cutler
> Naval Institute Press, Annapolis, MD, 2017.

Character in Action: The U.S. Coast Guard on Leadership
> Donald T. Phillips and ADM James M. Loy, USCG (Ret.)
> Naval Institute Press, Annapolis, MD, 2003.

Command at Sea, 6th Edition
> ADM James Stavridis, USN (Ret.), and RADM Robert
> Girrier, USN (Ret.)
> Naval Institute Press, Annapolis, MD, 2010.

"Commandant Instruction M5351.3: Leadership Development
Framework"
> Commandant, U.S. Coast Guard
> Department of Homeland Security, Washington, DC,
> May 2006.

Division Officer's Guide, 12th Edition
> ADM James Stavridis, USN (Ret.) and RADM Robert
> Girrier USN (Ret.) with CDR Jeffrey Heames, USN and
> CDR Thomas Ogden, USN
> Naval Institute Press, Annapolis, MD, 2017.

Fundamentals of Naval Leadership
> Department of Leadership and Law, U.S. Naval Academy
> Edited by Prof. Karel Montor and Maj Anthony J. Ciotti,
> USMC
> Naval Institute Press, Annapolis, MD, 1984.

Leadership Embodied, 2nd Edition: The Secrets to Success of the Most Effective Navy and Marine Corps Leaders
> Edited by LtCol Joseph J. Thomas
> Naval Institute Press, Annapolis, MD, 2013.

Naval Leadership: Voices of Experience
> Edited by Karel Montor; CAPT Thomas McNicholas, USN; LtCol Anthony Ciotti, USMC; LCDR Thomas Hutchinson, USNR; and Jackie Eckhart Wehmueller
> Naval Institute Press, Annapolis, MD, 1998.

The Naval Officer's Guide, 13th Edition
> CDR Lesa A. McComas, USN (Ret.), and CDR J. D. Kristenson, USN
> Naval Institute Press, Annapolis, MD, 2019.

Navy Leader Planning Guide
> Center for Personal and Professional Development, Norfolk, 2010.

Leadership Books from Other Services

The Armed Forces Officer
> US Department of Defense
> National Defense University Press and Potomac Books, Washington, DC, 2007.

Army Leadership and the Profession
> U.S. Army Field Manual 6-22 (FM 22-100)
> Headquarters, Department of the Army,
> Washington DC, 2015. (July 2019)

Department of Homeland Security Coast Guard Leadership Competencies
> https://www.dcms.uscg.mil/Portals/10/CG-1/leadership/docs/pdf/competencies1.pdf?ver=2017-03-22-114340-870.

Ethics and the Military Profession: Moral Foundations of Leadership
> (Fifth Edition)
> Edited by Dr. George R. Lucas Jr. and CAPT W. Rick Rubel, USN (Ret.)
> Pearson/Longman, Boston, 2014.

Leading Marines
> Field Manual FMFM 1-0
> DON
> HQ USMC, 1995.

Muddy Boots Leadership: Real-Life Stories and Personal Examples of Good, Bad, and Unexpected Results
> MAJ John Chapman, USA
> Stackpole Books, Mechanicsburg, PA, 2006.

Leadership Books from Business and Academia

AMA Handbook of Leadership
> Marshall Goldsmith, John Baldoni, and Sarah McArthur
> American Management Association, New York, 2010.

Churchill on Leadership
> Steven F. Hayward
> Three Rivers Press, New York, 1998.

The Contrarian's Guide to Leadership
> Stephen B. Sample and Warren Bennis
> Jossey-Bass, San Francisco, 2003.

The Effective Executive: The Definitive Guide to Getting the Right Things Done, 50th Anniversary Edition
> Peter F. Drucker
> Harper Business, New York, 2017.

It's Your Ship, 10th Anniversary Edition
> CAPT D. Michael Abrashoff
> Warner Books, New York, 2012.

The Leadership Challenge: How to Keep Getting Extraordinary Things Done in Organizations, 6th Edition
    James M. Kouzes and Barry Z. Posner
    Jossey-Bass, San Francisco, 2017.

Leadership: Enhancing the Lessons of Experience, 9th Edition
    Richard L. Hughes, Robert C. Ginnett, Gordon J. Curphy
    McGraw-Hill Irwin, Boston, 2018.

Leadership for Dummies
    Dr. John Marrin
    John Wiley and Sons, Ltd, Chichester, UK, 2011.

The Leadership Lessons of Jesus: A Timeless Model for Today's Leaders
    Bob Briner and Ray Pritchard
    Broadman & Holman, Nashville, TN, 2008.

Leadership Lessons of the White House Fellows: Learn How to Inspire Others, Achieve Greatness, and Find Success in Any Organization
    Charles P. Garcia
    McGraw-Hill, New York, 2009.

Leadership Mastery: How to Challenge Yourself and Others to Greatness
    Dale Carnegie Training
    Simon & Schuster, New York, 2009.

The Nature of Leadership, 3rd Edition
    Edited by John Antonakis, Anna T. Cianciolo, and
    Robert J. Sternberg
    SAGE Publications, Thousand Oaks, CA, 2017.

Patton on Leadership
    Alan Axelrod
    Prentice Hall, Paramus, NJ, 2001.

Preparing to Lead: Principles of Self-Leadership and Organizational Dynamics, 8th Edition
    CDR Arthur Gibb, USN
    Pearson Education, Boston, 2009.

The Rules of Management: A Definitive Code for Managerial Success, 4th Edition
    Richard Templar
    Pearson Prentice Hall, New Jersey, 2015.

Semper Fi: Business Leadership the Marine Corps Way
    Dan Carrison and Rod Walsh
    Amacom, New York, 2004.

Successful Executive's Handbook
    Susan H. Gebelein, David G. Lee, Kristie J. Nelson-Heuhaus, and Elaine B. Sloan
    Personnel Decisions International Corporation, Minneapolis, 1999.

The Transformational Leader, 2nd Edition
    Noel M. Tichy and Mary Anne DeVanna
    John Wiley & Sons, New York, 1997.

The 21 Indispensable Qualities of a Leader: Becoming the Person Others Will Want to Follow
    John C. Maxwell
    Thomas Nelson, Nashville, TN, 2012.

A CONVERSATION WITH THE AGES

Imagine as a young officer being able to somehow stand in a room with Washington, Jefferson, Paine, Churchill, Einstein, Saint Paul, Carnegie, and Theodore Roosevelt. Imagine if they were joined by military and naval heroes, including Patton, John Paul Jones, Burke, Nimitz, and Eisenhower, and by other thought leaders, CEOs, and philosophers.

What might such a group say about leadership?

Let's bring you into that Room of the Ages and ask three leadership questions to the assembled group of luminaries. It might go like this. (Remember, the three questions asked are ours, but the answers are all direct quotes from the sayings or writings of the luminaries listed.)

Question 1: "What do you believe is the MOST IMPORTANT LEADERSHIP ATTRIBUTE?"

GEN ALEXANDER PATCH: The foundation of leadership is *character*.

GEN H. NORMAN SCHWARZKOPF: Leadership is a potent combination of strategy and *character*. But if you must be without one, be without the strategy.

GEN GEORGE S. PATTON: *Moral courage* is the most valuable and usually the most absent characteristic in men.

WINSTON CHURCHILL: *Courage* is rightly esteemed the first of human qualities . . . because it is the quality that guarantees all others.

SAM WALTON: *High expectations* are the key to everything.

NAPOLEON: Be *clear,* be clear, be clear.

TONY BLAIR: The art of leadership is saying "no," not "yes." It is very easy to say "yes."

EUGENE B. HABECKER, AUTHOR: The true leader *serves.* Serves people. Serves their best interests, and in so doing will not always be popular, may not always impress. But because true leaders are motivated by loving concern rather than a desire for personal glory, they are willing to pay the price.

STEPHEN GREGG, CHAIRMAN AND CEO, ETHIX CORPORA- TION: People do not follow uncommitted leaders. *Commitment* can be displayed in a full range of matters to include the work hours you choose to maintain, how you work to improve your abilities, or what you do for your fellow workers at personal sacrifice.

CONRAD HILTON: Success seems to be connected with *action.* Successful people keep moving. They make mistakes, but they don't quit.

THEODORE ROOSEVELT: The most important single ingredient in the formula of success is *knowing how to get along with people.*

SUN TZU: By command I mean the general's qualities of *wisdom, sincerity, humanity, courage,* and *strictness.*

DENIS WAITLEY, AUTHOR: The winner's edge is not in a gifted birth, a high IQ, or in talent. The winner's edge is all in the *attitude,* not aptitude. Attitude is the criterion for success.

HENRY GRULAND, BUSINESSMAN: Being a leader is more than just wanting to lead. Leaders have *empathy* for others and a keen ability to find the best in people . . . not the worst . . . by truly caring for others.

LEE IACOCCA: I have found that *being honest* is the best technique I can use. Right up front, tell people what you're trying to accomplish and what you're willing to sacrifice to accomplish it.

KEN BLANCHARD: The only way to develop *responsibility* in people is to give them responsibility.

SAMUEL JOHNSON: *Self-confidence* is the first requisite to great undertakings.

VADM JAMES STOCKDALE: The test of character is not "hanging in there" when you expect a light at the end of the tunnel, but *performance of duty and persistence* of example when you know that no light is coming.

ALBERT EINSTEIN: *Setting an example* is not the main means of influencing another; it is the only means.

DAVID LEE: *Communication* is the currency of leadership.

WARREN BENNIS: Many leaders do not have *empathy*, but . . . those that lack empathy lack the ability to move people. Leaders who can instill an atmosphere of working together gain respect, taking charge without taking control.

GEN PATTON: I can tell a commander by the way he *speaks*. He does not have to swear as much as I do, but he has to speak so that no one will refuse to follow his order.

CARLY FIORINA, CEO, HEWLETT-PACKARD: There is no substitute for *hard work*. It will always outweigh brilliance over time.

LEE IACOCCA: If I had to sum up in one word what makes a good manager, I'd say *decisiveness*.

Question 2: "What other LEADERSHIP ADVICE do you have for me to consider?"

RADM GRACE HOPPER: You don't manage people; you manage things. You lead people.

GEN GEORGE S. PATTON: You young lieutenants have to realize that your platoon is like a piece of spaghetti. You can't push it. You've got to get out in front and pull it.

ADM ARLEIGH "31-KNOT" BURKE: There must be a common purpose or there can be no success.

GEN COLIN POWELL: There are no secrets to success. It is the result of preparation, hard work, and learning from failure.

ANONYMOUS SEAGOING OFFICER: You get what you inspect, not what you expect!

ADM BURKE: It is imperative for . . . an officer to know his sailors. Get to know them—know their strengths, their weaknesses, their skills, their wisdom.

SOLON: Learn to obey before you command.

ADM THOMAS H. MOORER: A leader can gain the support of his people by telling them specifically what should and should not be done. People do not like receiving orders that leave them uncertain of what is required of them.

WILLIAM BUTLER YEATS: Think like a wise man but communicate in the language of the people.

SAINT PAUL: Whatsoever thou doeth, do it with all thy might.

CAPT DANIEL GLADE, USA: [You] have to be the unit's leader or commander. To do that you cannot be one of the troops. They do not need another buddy. They need a leader and expect you will step up to that. Be demanding on standards and tough-minded in the way you decide and conduct yourself. Care for your troops but be a leader.

Standing order from HQ to a Coast Guard leader in the field: Do what you have to do. Act first. Call me later.

Albert Einstein: Make everything as simple as possible, but not simpler.

Andrew Carnegie: No man will make a great leader who wants to do it all himself, or to get all the credit for doing it.

Mary Browne: Expect people to be better than they are; it helps them to become better. But don't be disappointed when they are not; it helps them to keep trying.

Mary Kay Ash: Sandwich every bit of criticism between two layers of praise.

ADM Chester Nimitz: First, determine what career you want to follow, then plan it all the way to the top. Then ask for the best and toughest job available that suits your career path.

Walter Lippmann: The genius of a good leader is to leave behind him a situation which common sense, without the trace of genius, can deal with successfully.

Winston Churchill: There is great wisdom in reserving one's decision as long as possible and until all the facts and forces that will be potent at the moment are revealed.

ADM Burke: If the equipment doesn't work in battle, it doesn't make much difference how much else the officers know, the battle is lost—and so are the people in it.

So—it can be right handy to be a good engineer first—
and a brilliant theorist after.

MARY WALDROP: It's important that people know what you
stand for. It's equally important that they know what
you won't stand for.

GEN H. NORMAN SCHWARZKOPF: Rule 13: When put into a
position of command, take charge. Rule 14: When put
into a position of command, do what is right.

DWIGHT D. EISENHOWER: You do not lead by hitting people over the head—that's assault, not leadership.

JESSE JACKSON: Leadership cannot just go along to get along.
Leadership must meet the moral challenge of the day.

RICHARD THORNBURGH: Subordinates cannot be left to
speculate as to the values of the organization. Top leadership must give forth clear and explicit signals, lest any
confusion or uncertainty exist over what is and is not
permissible conduct.

GEN PATTON: When a decision has to be made, make it.
There is no totally right time for anything.

BENJAMIN DISRAELI: Nurture your mind with great
thoughts. To believe in the heroic makes heroes.

GEN PATTON: Commanders must remember that the issu-
ance of an order, or the devising of a plan, is only about
5 percent of the responsibility of command. The other
95 percent is to ensure, by personal observation . . . that
the order is carried out.

SAINT JAMES: Be swift to hear, slow to speak, slow to wrath.

MARGARET A. WHEATLEY: Power in an organization is the
capacity generated by relationships.

PETER DRUCKER: If you can't measure it, then you can't
manage it.

WALTER LIPPMANN: The final test of a leader is that he leaves behind him in other men the conviction and the will to carry on.

SAINT AMBROSE: The wise man, before he speaks, will consider well what he speaks, to whom he speaks, and where and when.

GEN PATTON: There is a great deal of talk about loyalty from the bottom to the top. Loyalty from the top down is even more necessary and much less prevalent.

DONALD T. REGAN: You've got to give loyalty down, if you want loyalty up.

SENECA: He who has great power should use it lightly.

MARGARET CHASE SMITH: One of the basic causes for all the trouble in the world today is that people talk too much and think too little. They act impulsively without thinking. I always try to think before I talk.

WINSTON CHURCHILL: An accepted leader has only to be sure of what it is best to do, or at least to have made up his mind about it.

B. H. LIDDEL HART: A commander should have a profound understanding of human nature, the knack of smoothing out troubles, the power of winning affection while communicating energy, and the capacity for ruthless determination where required by circumstances. He needs to generate an electrifying current, and to keep a cool head in applying it.

THOMAS JEFFERSON: I am a great believer in luck, and I find the harder I work the more I have of it.

GEN JOHN LEJEUNE: The relation between officers and men should in no sense be that of superior and inferior nor that of master and servant, but rather that of teacher and scholar.

THEODORE ROOSEVELT: The best executive is one who has sense enough to pick good people to do what he wants done, and self-restraint enough to keep from meddling with them while they do it.

GEN PATTON: Never tell people how to do things. Tell them what to do and they will surprise you with their ingenuity.

WINSTON CHURCHILL: Ponder, and then *act*.

JOHANN WOLFGANG VON GOETHE: Correction does much, but encouragement does more. Encouragement after censure is as the sun after a shower.

HARRY TRUMAN: It's amazing how much you can accomplish if you do not care who gets the credit.

GEN WILLIAM T. SHERMAN: The true way to be popular with troops is not to be free and familiar with them, but to make them believe you know more than they do.

AMOS BRONSON ALCOTT: First find the man in yourself if you will inspire manliness in others.

RALPH WALDO EMERSON: Trust men, and they will be true to you.

THEODORE ROOSEVELT: Nobody cares how much you know, until they know how much you care.

MARY DEE HICKS: When you're in a new job where you're stretched, your focus should be on learning, not getting an A.

JOHN BUCHAN: The task of leadership is not to put greatness into humanity, but to elicit it, for the greatness is already there.

ERNEST HEMINGWAY: When people talk, listen completely. Most people never listen.

GEN SCHWARZKOPF: Every substandard organization I have ever seen had low performance standards. If you want superior performance, then you have got to set high standards.

WELSH PROVERB: He that would be a leader must be a bridge.

VADM JAMES STOCKDALE: Strange as it sounds, great leaders gain authority by giving it away.

JOHN C. MAXWELL: Competence goes beyond words. It's the leader's ability to say it, plan it, and do it in such a way that others know you know how—and know that they want to follow you.

THEODORE ROOSEVELT: Do what you can, where you are at, with what you have.

CONFUCIUS: Respect yourself and others will respect you.

ADM BURKE: Success cannot be administered.

LORD NELSON: Recollect that you must be a seaman to be an officer; and also that you cannot be a good officer without being a gentleman.

JOHN W. WEEKS, FORMER SECRETARY OF WAR: "An officer and a gentleman" is a familiar term to everyone both in and out of the Service. Be sure you are both. You cannot be an officer and a gentleman unless you are just, humane, thoroughly trained, unless you have character, a high sense of honor, and an unselfish devotion to duty. Be an example of such to everyone.

XENOPHON: No one can be a good officer who does not undergo more than those he commands.

JOHN C. MAXWELL: A good leader encourages followers to tell him what he needs to know, not what he wants to hear.

"What are your thoughts on making MISTAKES?"

ELBERT HUBBARD, AUTHOR: The greatest mistake one can make in life is to be continually fearing you will make one.

THEODORE ROOSEVELT: The only man who never makes a mistake is the man who never does anything.

WESTON H. AGOR: Making mistakes simply means you are learning faster.

DAVID B. PETERSON: The more you crash, the more you learn.

DR. LINUS PAULING: The best way to have a good idea is to have a lot of ideas.

THOMAS WATSON SR., FOUNDER OF IBM: The fastest way to succeed is to double the failure rate.

GEN BRUCE C. CLARKE: You must be able to underwrite the honest mistakes of your subordinates if you wish to develop their initiative and experience.

ROBERT F. KENNEDY: Only those who dare to fail greatly can ever achieve greatly.

THEODORE ROOSEVELT: He who makes no mistakes, makes no progress.

INDEX

Abrashoff, Michael, 162–63
accountability: captain's, Kacher
    on near collision and,
    140–42; Mustin on viewing
    delegation compared with,
    68; Tomney on offshore
    party and, 112–14
action plan, for TEAMS model,
    183–85
Adams, John, 17
Adelman, Ken, 6
Administration Office, Pendley
    on caring for Sailors and,
    118–20
adversity, as leadership building
    block, 11
advice from those who have led:
    The Bluejacket's Manual,
    162; *The Contrarian's Guide
    to Leadership*, 166–67; *The
    Division Officer's Guide*,
    160–61; *The Effective Exec-
    utive*, 167–68; Hamilton on
    leadership, 155; historical
    leaders on, 196–202; *It's
    Your Ship*, 162–63; *The
    Leadership Challenge*,
    169–70; *Leadership Mastery:
    How to Challenge Yourself
    and Others to Greatness*,
    166; *Leading Marines*, 164;
    Muddy Boots Leadership,
    163; *Navy Leader Plan-
    ning Guide*, 161; overview,
    155–56; *Semper Fi: Business
    Leadership the Marine Corps
    Way*, 164–65
Agor, Weston H., 202

aircraft carrier, man overboard
    from, 90–93
alcohol: Coane on master chief's
    problem with, 128–29; at
    offshore party, Tomney on
    aftermath of, 112–14
Alcott, Amos Bronson, 200
all stop, Rewkowski on judicious
    use of, 144–46
AMA Handbook of Leadership
    (American Management
    Association), 44–45, 189
Amazon.com, leadership books
    on, 24
Ambrose, Saint, 199
anchoring scenario, Rewkowski
    on all stop in, 144–46
answers, Sadler on not having all
    the, 129–30
Armed Forces Officer, The, 33,
    40, 188
Army, on leadership, 4–5. See
    also *U.S. Army Leadership
    Field Manual*
Art of War, The (Sun Tzu), 15
Ash, Mary Kay, 197
Asimakopoulos, Aaron, 146–47
Athens, Art, 10–11
attitude, in TEAMS model, 182,
    183, 184
attributes and traits of leaders,
    books on: *The Armed Forces
    Officer*, 33; *Character in
    Action*, 32; *Churchill on
    Leadership*, 37; *Command
    at Sea*, 31–32; consensus of
    lists on, 28–29; *Fundamen-
    tals of Naval Leadership*, 30;

49–51; Great Man theory and, 16; leadership advice, 201; on performance of duty and persistence, 195

stories, organizational, 112

strong people, leadership and, 9

study of leadership: elements in, 15; in long-term SPOM game plan, 177–78; Soukhanov on competency development and, 153–54. *See also* SPOM: Study, Practice, Observe, Mentor

subordinates: 360-degree feedback from, 176. *See also* followers; Sailors

Successful Executive's Handbook (Gebelein, Lee, Nelson-Heuhaus, and Sloan), 43–44, 191

Sullivan, Kathy: leadership model of, 172–73, 174; one-page plan of, 179–80

Sun Tzu, 15, 194

surveys, 360-degree feedback, 176

symbols, organizational, 112

tactical action officer (TAO), Quinn (warfighter XO) as, 147–48

taking care of people: Boxall on mistakes in, 82–83; Christenson on fortune favoring the bold, 80–81; Dixon on the Sailor and his son, 87–89; as foundation of leadership, 75; Henderson on man overboard, 90–93; Herbert on prisoner and, 75–77; leaders on, 74; Ledford on leadership by unintentional example,

131–32; Maver-Shue on building esprit de corps, 86–87; Norton on knowing your people, 77–78; racist statements and, 79; Rowden on command advancing a Sailor, 83–84; Sisk on danger to life and health, 95–96; Timme on the Ensign in the snow, 93–94; Wray on a sinking ship and, 84–85; Wray on safety first, 89–90

tall people, leadership and, 9

tanker tie-up, Asimakopoulos on bird-caged wire during, 146–47

task-oriented leaders, Contingency theory and, 19

team work (competencies): as desirable leadership trait, 158–60; professional competence and, 134–35; Sadler on not having all the answers and, 129–30; in TEAMS model, 182, 184

TEAMS model: action plan, 183–85; elements in, 182–83

Thornburgh, Richard, 198

360-degree feedback, 176

Thucydides, 15

Timme, William, 93–94

Title 10, U.S. Code, on leadership, 24

Tomney, Christopher, 112–14

Toti, William, 151–53

training your relief, Roberts on, 135–37

traits, leadership: Great Man theory and, 16–17; in a junior officer, sea-service survey on, 157; as learned, 9–10; most and least

ABOUT THE AUTHORS

RADM Robert O. Wray Jr., USN (Ret.), a U.S. Naval Academy graduate, served as a nuclear engineer on surface ships. After transferring to the Navy Reserve, he enjoyed a multi-faceted career in construction, hospitality, and technology. After promotion to admiral, he returned to active duty for six years. He is now CEO of a tech company in Maryland.

CDR Andrew Ledford, USN, PhD, graduated from the U.S. Naval Academy in 1995 and spent his first four years in the military as a Marine Infantry Officer. He later transferred to the Navy where he led operational units in austere regions around the world. In 2013 he was selected to be a Permanent Military Professor for the Navy. He went on to receive his PhD from Princeton University and currently teaches leadership at the Naval Academy in Annapolis, Maryland.

VADM John B. Mustin, USN, hailing from a distinguished Navy family, is a surface warfare officer with afloat service on Aegis cruisers and destroyers, and command experience at the O-4, O-5, O-6, and Strike Group level. As Commander, Expeditionary Strike Group TWO, he led fourteen ships, ten ashore commands, and 25,000 sailors and Marines. He currently serves as the Chief of Navy Reserve.

RDML Theodore P. S. LeClair, USN, is from Scituate, Massachusetts, a small coastal town. A Villanova University NROTC alum, RDML LeClair is a surface warfare officer with operational experience in the Atlantic, Pacific, and Indian Oceans, as well as the Mediterranean Sea and Arabian Gulf. He has command experience at the O-4, O-5, and O-6 level. As Deputy Commander, U.S. Seventh Fleet, he helped lead the largest forward deployed naval force in the world. He currently serves as the Deputy Director for Operations, U.S. Indo-Pacific Command.

The Naval Institute Press is the book-publishing arm of the U.S. Naval Institute, a private, nonprofit, membership society for sea service professionals and others who share an interest in naval and maritime affairs. Established in 1873 at the U.S. Naval Academy in Annapolis, Maryland, where its offices remain today, the Naval Institute has members worldwide.

Members of the Naval Institute support the education programs of the society and receive the influential monthly magazine *Proceedings* or the colorful bimonthly magazine *Naval History* and discounts on fine nautical prints and on ship and aircraft photos. They also have access to the transcripts of the Institute's Oral History Program and get discounted admission to any of the Institute-sponsored seminars offered around the country.

The Naval Institute's book-publishing program, begun in 1898 with basic guides to naval practices, has broadened its scope to include books of more general interest. Now the Naval Institute Press publishes about seventy titles each year, ranging from how-to books on boating and navigation to battle histories, biographies, ship and aircraft guides, and novels. Institute members receive significant discounts on the Press' more than eight hundred books in print.

Full-time students are eligible for special half-price membership rates. Life memberships are also available.

For a free catalog describing Naval Institute Press books currently available, and for further information about joining the U.S. Naval Institute, please write to:

Member Services
U.S. Naval Institute
291 Wood Road
Annapolis, MD 21402-5034
Telephone: (800) 233-8764
Fax: (410) 571-1703
Web address: www.usni.org